Persian proverbs' effects on Urdu language

(*A Paremiologic Research*)

A. A. Abedian K.

Book's Name:	Persian proverbs' effects on Urdu language (A paremiologic research)
Author:	**Abedian Kasgari, Ali Akbar, 1958 -**
ISBN:	9781979549059
Publisher:	Degarandishan Publishing House
Edited By:	Morvarid Abedian Kasgari

Paremiologic Research Number: 11

Parts of this paremiologic research is presented in the scientific and cultural conference of Paremiologists *(10th International Conference of Paremiology - Interdisciplinary Colloquia on Proverbs -ICP16-)* held by AIP-IAP in November 2016 (Tavira – Portugal)

AIP-IAP (International Association of Paremiology) is a non-profit cultural institution based in Tavira (Algarve, Portugal). The quality of the AIP-IAP are recognized by experts in the proverbial thematic, especially for Paremiologists and Phraseologists of world worthy. This dynamism in the collection, preservation and dissemination of intangible cultural heritage, has led the United Nations Educational, Scientific and Cultural Organization (UNESCO), the Ministry of Culture-Regional Delegation of the Algarve, the City Council of Tavira (CMT), the Foundation for Science and Technology (FCT) and the Cultural Centre in Lisbon to support the initiatives of the *AIP-IAP.*

Contents

فهرست ضرب‌المثل‌های فارسی

(فارسی کهاوتیں کے انڈیکس)

f

<h1 style="text-align:center">اردو کہاوتیں کے انڈیکس</h1>

(فہرست ضرب‌المثل‌های اردو)

Persian Proverbs
(in Phonemic/Alphabetical Order)

Persian Phonemes	Page
/ɒːb o ɒːtæʃ bə hæm næjɒːjæd rɒːst/	109-111
/ɒːb o ɒːtæʃ rɒː hæGiːr mæʃmɒːr/	107
/ɒːb o ɒːtæʃ rɒː t͡ʃæ ɒːʃænɒːiː/	109
/ɒːb o ɒːtæʃ χælɒːfə jədəgærænd/	111
/ɒːləmə biː æmæl mɒːnændə dəræχtə biː sæmær æst/	162
/ɒːləmiː rɒː kə goft bɒːʃæd o bæs/ – /hær t͡ʃə guːjæd nægiːræd ændær kæs/	162
/ɒːn kæs æst æhl ə bəʃɒːræt kə əʃɒːræt dɒːnæd/	160
/ɒːtæʃ ægær ændæk æst hæGiːr næbɒːjæd dɒːʃt/	107
/æd͡ʒælə kɒːr ə ʃəjtɒːn æst/	152
/ægær goftæn siːm æst χɒːmuːʃiː zær æst/	145
/æsbə næd͡ʒiːb rɒː jək tɒːzjɒːnə bæs æst/	129
/æz goftænə ɒːtæʃ zæbɒːn næsuːzæd/	114
/bɒːdænd͡ʒɒːn bɒːd dɒːræd bæliː nædɒːræd bæliː/	104
/bæd rɒː bɒːjæd bæd goft χuːb rɒː χuːb/	123
/bærɒːj ə kuːr ʃæb o ruːz jəkiː æst/	133

/bæχt ə bæd sæg gæzæd/	135
/bæχt t͡ʃon bærgæʃt pɒːluːdəh dændɒːn bəʃkænæd/	135
/bəhəʃt ziːr ə pɒːj ə mɒːdærɒːn æst/	147
/biːgɒːriː bəh kə biːkɒːriː/	148
/buːd͡ʒɒːr ə lənd͡ʒɒːn æst hær suː bɒːd mi ɒːjæd bɒːd miː dæhæd/	104
/dær hæmiːʃə bə jək pɒːʃnə nəmiː gærdæd/	173
/dær ʃæhr ə kuːrɒːn mærd ə jək t͡ʃəʃm pɒːdəʃɒːh æst/	132
/diːgiː kə bærɒːjə mæn næd͡ʒuːʃæd særə sæg dær ɒːn bəd͡ʒuːʃæd/	133
/do duːzə miː bɒːzæd/	166
/do pɒːdəʃɒːh dær əGliːmiː nægonjænd/	137
/do ʃæmʃiːr dær nəjɒːmiː nægonjæd/	137
/dorrə dærə χəlɒːb hæm dor æst/	175
/duːst ɒːn bɒːʃæd kə giːræd dæst ə duːst/	176
/duːstiː ə χɒːlə χərsə/	168
/əhtjɒːd͡ʒ mɒːdær ə əχtərɒːʔ æst/	159
/færdɒː rɒː kə diːdə æst/	163
/Gærz məGrɒːzə mohæbbæt æst/	127

/Gærz ʃuːjə mærdɒːn æst/	127
/gorosnə dæ χɒːb nɒːnə sængæk miː biːnæd/	165
/hær d͡ʒɒː goliː æst χɒːriː dær pæhluːjə uːst/	155
/hær d͡ʒɒː kə pæriː roχiː æst diːviː bɒː uːst/	155
/hær kæsiː χodɒːiː dɒːræd – Gəsmæti jodɒːiː dɒːræd/	150
/hær t͡ʃə dəlæm χɒːst næh ɒːn miː ʃævæd/ - /hær t͡ʃə χodɒː χɒːst hæmɒːn miː ʃævæd/	144
/hiːt͡ʃ duːdi biː ɒːtæʃiː niːst/	112
/jək dæst sədɒː nædɒːræd/	138
/kɒːr ə əmruz bə færdɒː mæfəkæn/	106
/kæm bəχor hæmiːʃə bəχor/	164
/kæs næguːjæd kə duːɣ ə mæn torʃ æst/	118
/kolæh ə æhmæd rɒː sær ə mæhmuːd gozɒːʃtæn/	125
/kolæh ə æhmæd sær ə mæhmuːd/	125
/kuːr ə χod æst o biːnɒːjə mærdom/	103
/mæn nokær ə hɒːkəmæm næ nokær ə bɒːdənd͡ʒɒːn/	104
/moʒə bə t͡ʃæʃm zjɒːdæti nækonæd/	116
/nɒːbordə rænd͡ʒ gænd͡ʒ mojæssær nəmiː ʃævæd/	156

/nɒːmə bolænd bəhtær æz bɒːmə bolænd æst/	170
/niːm hækiːm bælɒːjə jɒːn/ – /niːm fæGiːh bælɒːjə iːmɒːn/	171
/porsɒːn porsɒːn bə kææbə miː tævɒːn ræft/	149
/porsɒːn porsɒːn miːrævænd (bə) hənduːstɒːn/	149
/puːl æst næ d͡ʒɒːn æst kə ɒːsɒːn bətævɒːn dɒːd/	175
/ruːbəruː d͡ʒɒːnæm d͡ʒɒːnæt poʃtə sær kɒːrdɒːm ostəχɒːnæt/	166
/sæg dær ə χɒːnəjə sɒːhəbæʃ ʃiːr æst/	119
/sælɒːm ə ruːstɒːiː biː tæmæʔ niːst/	141
/sæliːGə hɒː moχtæləf æst/	174
/sæʔdiːɒː mærd ə nəkuːnɒːm næmiːræd hærgəz/ – /mordə ɒːn æst kə nɒːmæʃ bə nəkuːiː næbæ"rænd/	170
/ʃotor dær χɒːb biːnæd pænbə dɒːnə/ – /gæhiː lop lop xoræd gæh dɒːnə dɒːnə/	165
/tɒː nægərjæd æbr kəj χændæd t͡ʃæmæn/	142
/tɒː nægərjæd təfl kəj nuːʃæd/	142
/t͡ʃə bærɒːj ə kuːr bəzæniː t͡ʃə bəræGsiː/	133
/t͡ʃuːb ə χodɒː sədɒː nædɒːræd/	131
/χodɒː kæs ə biːkæsɒːn æst/	151

/χodɒː væGtiː miː dæhæd nəmiː porsæd kiːstiː/	150
/χodkærdə rɒː tædbiːr niːst/	121
/χod rɒː fæsiːhæt, digærɒːn rɒː næsiːhæt/	103
/χod zəndə, d͡ʒæhɒːn zəndə – χod mordə, d͡ʒæhɒːn mordə/	101
/zæbɒːnæm kə næsuːχt/	114
/zuːræʃ bə χær nəmiː rəsæd pɒːlɒːnæʃ rɒː miːzænæd/	178

Urdu Proverbs
(in Phonemic/Alphabetical Order)

/ædhɒ:r mohæbbæt ki: Gi:nt͡ʃi: hə/	127
/æGlmænd ko i:k əʃɒ:ræ kɒ:fi: hə/	160
/æhmæd ki: pægæri: mæhmu:d ki: sær/	125
/ællɒ:h ki: lɒ:thi: məjn ɒ:vɒ:z nəhi:n̪/	131
/æmæl ki: bə ɣəjrə əlm bi: pəhəl dəræχt ki: mɒ:nænd hə/	162
/ændhi: ku:dən rɒ:t bærɒ:bər/	133
/ændhu:n məjn kɒ:nɒ: rɒ:d͡ʒɒ:/	132
/æʃrɒ:f ghu:ri: ku: t͡ʃɒ:bu:k ki: hɒ:d͡ʒæt nəhi:n̪/	129
/æt͡ʃhi: ku: æt͡ʃhɒ: bəri: ku: bærɒ: kəhti: həjn̪/	123
/bændi: kɒ: t͡ʃæhɒ:kt͡ʃə nəhi:n̪ hotɒ:/ - /ællɒ:h kɒ: t͡ʃəhɒ: səb kət͡ʃə hotɒ: hə/	144
/bəhəʃt mɒ:n ki: Gædæmu:n təki: hə/	147
/bən ru:i: mɒ:n bəhi: du:du nəhi:n̪ dəjti:/	142
/bəni: kɒ: sælɒ:m bi: ɣæræz nəhi:n̪ hotɒ:/	141
/bi:kɒ:ri: si: bi:gɒ:ri: bəhli:/	148
/bu:lnɒ: t͡ʃɒ:ndi: hə mægær ræhnɒ: su:nɒ: hə/	145

/d͡ʒæhɒːn guːl hogɒː væhɒːn χɒːr bəhiː zæruːr hogɒː/	155
/d͡ʒæhɒːn gæn͡dʒ væhɒːn ræn͡dʒ /	156
/d͡ʒældiː kɒː kæm ʃəjtɒːn kɒː/	153
/d͡ʒəb χuːdɒː dəjniː pær ɒːtɒː hə tuːphərjə nəhiːn̪ kəhtɒː kə tuː kon hə/	150
/d͡ʒəs kɒː koiː nəhiːn̪ əs kɒː χuːdɒː/	151
/əjk hɒːtə siː tɒːliː nəhiːn̪ bəd͡ʒətiː/	138
/əjk məjɒːn məjn do təlvɒːr nəhiːn̪ rəh sækt/	137
/hær ʃæχs kɒː məzɒːd͡ʒ moχtæləf huːtɒː hə/	174
/jær kɒː ɣossæ bəhtɒːr kiː uːppər/	178
/jærohiː d͡ʒo bəhiːr məin̪ kɒːm ɒːiː/	176
/jərɒː kiːt͡ʃər məin̪ bəhiː hiːrɒː rətɒː hə/	175
/kæl kæs niː dəjkhiː hə/	163
/kæm kæhɒː ɣæm nə kæhɒː/	164
/mən məjn bæsiː dəspəniː dæsiː/	165
/mənə pər or piːtə piːt͡ʃiː or/	166

/nɒːdɒːn kiː dostiː d͡ʒiː kɒː zjɒːn/	168
/nɒːmə bolænd bəh æz bɒːmə bolænd/	170
/niːm hækiːm χætær ə jɒːn/ – /niːm muːllɒː χætær ə iːmɒːn/	171
/puːt͡ʃhti puːt͡ʃhti χuːdɒː kɒː Gæhær məl d͡ʒɒːtɒː hə/	149
/uːnt t͡ʃærhiː kətɒː kɒːthiː/	135
/væGt hæməʃæ əjk sɒː nəhiːn rətɒː/	173
/zəruːræt iːd͡ʒɒːd kiː mɒːn hə/	159

English Equivalents
(in Alphabetical Order)

Proverb	Page
A dripping June sets all in tune	143
A friend in need is a friend indeed	176
A little knowledge is a dangerous thing	172
A little learning is a dangerous thing	171
A nod is as good as a wink	134
A nod's as good as a wink to a blind horse	133
A penny saved is a penny earned	164
A word to the wise	160
A word to the wise is enough	129
After us the deluge	101
As you bake, so shall you brew	121
As you brew, so shall you bake	121
Better wear out than to rust out	147

It is a long lane that has no turning	173
It is not spring until you can plant your foot upon twelve daisies	142
It takes two to make a bargain	139
It takes two to make a quarrel	138
It takes two to tango	138
Judge not, that ye be not judged	103
Lend your money and lose your friend	127
Like lady, like maid	105
Like master, like man	104
Make haste slowly	152
Man proposes, God disposes	144
Man's extremity is God's opportunity	151
Many hands make light work	139
Money has no smell	175
More haste, less speed	153
Necessity is the mother of invention	159

To run with the hare and hunt with the hounds	166
To throw out the baby with the bathwater	169
Tomorrow never comes	163
Where God builds a church, the Devil will build a chapel	155
You can't put new wine in old bottles	109
You cannot run with the hare and hunt with the hounds	167

Introduction

Language is a social institution and its most important task is to create links between the communities. Language has long been considered by human as the oldest social phenomenon. Since some centuries B. C., when Panini 1 formulated some rules for Sanskrit language, the complex nature of language became the focus of attention of scholars. This kind of approach gradually led to the emergence of linguistics. Linguistics is a science that systematically examines language as an independent phenomenon. Linguists consider language as the easiest way to convey mental concepts and believe language is the simplest tool that one can use to communicate with others. Sometimes language is referred to as the key of the communication networks, and sometimes as means by which individuals can master it. For the thorough study of language, the intrinsic complexity of language led linguistics to study the descriptive and theoretical aspects of some other disciplines. One of the results of this evolution is the creation of an interdisciplinary domain called Applied Linguistics and a subfield called Paremiology which explores the proverbs. Proverbs are found in all languages, they are considered as part of folklore and social literature. Although proverbs may vary in terms of subjects and functions, it is generally accepted that the majority of the proverbs are adhered to certain social formations. Besides, regardless of the belonging languages, certain syntactic structures are based in the infrastructure of the proverbs. In fact paremiological surveys show that typical traditional examples about the proverbs are: X is Y; No X, no Y; Where there is X, there is Y; and Better X than Y. These syntactic structures or proverbial formulae which are in two

---

[1] Panini (4th century BC) is an ancient Sanskrit philologist, grammarian, and a revered scholar considered as the father of Indian linguistics.

fundamental affirmative and negative forms are found in Persian and Urdu proverbs as well, and are used together with other syntactic markers, phonological markers, and semantic markers as key parts of the proverbs.

One of the main events of the second millennium BC was the migration of people with Aryan origins to the Iranian plateau and the Indian-subcontinent. Although there are scholars who strongly reject the topic of the Aryans' migration and ascribe it as the basis for ethnic propaganda in favour of the European fascism, historical review of this book is prepared with regard to the popular belief of the Aryans' migration to these regions. Based on the former idea, after this migration, Indo-European family's language groups were formed, and the group of Iranian languages gradually stemmed out of the Indo-Iranian sub-family. Iranian languages besides to the Iranian Plateau, are native to the parts of the Caucasus, and much of Central Asia. With the existence of the Iranian languages' group and the formation of the Persian language, Persian started to improve as one of the main traits of the plateau's inhabitants. Based on historical divisions, linguists assign Iranian languages into three periods: *Ancient Era*, *Medieval Era*, and *New Era*. The distinct development in the transformation of the *Ancient Era* to the *Medieval Era* is changing of the synthetic form of the *Ancient Era* to an analytic form in the *Medieval Era*. The development in the transformation of the *Medieval Era* to the *New Era* were very gradual, and in the early phase of the New Persian, Middle Persian texts were still intelligible to speakers of New Persian in its early phase. However, there are definite differences that had taken place already by the 10th century. Sound changes such as: the dropping of unstressed initial vowels; the epenthesis of vowels in initial consonant clusters; the loss of -g when word finals; and change of initial w- to either b- or (gw- → g-). Changes in the verbal system, notably the loss of distinctive subjunctive and optative forms, and the increasing use of verbal prefixes to express verbal moods. Changes in the vocabulary, particularly the establishment of a superstratum or adstratum of Arabic loanwords replacing many Aramaic loans and native terms, and the substitution of Arabic script for Pahlavi script. Persian is the predominant modern descendant of Old Persian and is one of the Western Iranian languages within the Indo-Iranian branch of the Indo-European language family.

With a long history of literature, Persian was the first language in the Muslim world to break through Arabic's monopoly on writing, and the writing of poetry in Persian was established as a court tradition in many eastern courts including Urdu. Persian has had a considerable (mainly lexical) influence on neighboring languages, particularly the Turkic languages in Central Asia, Caucasus, and Anatolia, neighboring Iranian languages, as well as Armenian, Georgian, and Indo-Aryan languages, especially Urdu. For centuries, Persian has been a prestigious cultural language in other regions of Western Asia, Central Asia, and South Asia by the various empires based in the regions including Urdu speaking world. Following the Turko-Persian Ghaznavid conquest of South Asia, Persian was firstly introduced in the region by Turkic Central Asians. This lexically hybrid language, emerged in the northern subcontinent, was commonly called Zaban-e Urdu-e Mualla ('language of the exalted "army" camp') and eventually replaced Persian, the court language, and its name was shortened to just "Urdu". It grew from the interaction of Persian and Turkic-speaking Muslim soldiers and the native peoples. Under Persian influence from the state, the Persian and Nastaʿlīq scripts were adopted, with additional figures added to accommodate the Indo-Aryan phonetic system. Unlike Persian, which is an Iranian language, Urdu is an Indo-Aryan language2, written in the Persian alphabet, and contains

---

2 It is also claimed that Urdu is an Indo-European language, which does not have the same luxury, hence necessitating more memorization.

literary conventions and specialized vocabulary largely from Persian. Urdu plays a major role in the Muslim sphere of the western side of the subcontinent.

One of the major effects of the Persian language on the Urdu language is the influx of the Persian proverbs in Urdu, some of them without any changes. The book will provide a brief overview of the influence of the Persian language on the Urdu language and description of the usages of some Persian proverbs in Urdu language. To present the Persian proverbs, many sources such as Dehkhodā (1984), Farjam (1994), Habibian (2002), Ridout & Witting (2009), Ghanbari (2010), and Yousefi (2012) are surveyed, but the main source for the Persian quotations are from the masterpiece of the Persian proverbs, the researches of Ali Akbar Dehkhodā, a 20th century Persian Paremiologist.

To present the Urdu proverbs, many sources such as Datasy (1961), Firuz (1984), Geographical Names Romanization in Pakistan (1996), Kachru (2006), Naqavi (1988), Shebli (1997), and Morovvat (2007) are studied, but the main source for the Urdu quotations are quoted from the paremiologic works of Dr. Gholam Morovvat who has compared Urdu proverbs with the Persian equivalents.

To describe the research well, the English resembles of the proverbs are given in details, the English quotations quoted are from the works of Mawr (1885), Simpson (1985), Strauss (1994), and Manser (2007).

Notes on the book:

- The phonemes of the Persian proverbs are in /slashes/. These phonemes are written on the basis of the IPA system (The International Phonetic Alphabet). The standard Persian can not pronounce some Arabic sounds:

  "æ", and "ʔ" phonemes are as "æ",

  "tˤ", and "t" phonemes are as "t",

"θ", "sˤ", and "s" phonemes are as "s",

"ðˤ", "ð", "dˤ", and "z" phonemes are as "z",

"h", and "ħ" phonemes are as "h",

"ɟ", and "G" phonemes are as "G".

- As in Persian, consonants can be geminated, often in words from Arabic, in the IPA system this is represented by doubling the consonant, [səjjəd], or with the length marker ⟨ː⟩, [səjːəd]; in this book the first form is used.

To fulfill an appropriate introdution of the Persian language, many sources are surveyed but the main sources are: Paul, (2003) and Borjian (2015).

Although, English is not my native language, I have tried to survey the Persian proverbs' effects on the Urdu language, in English. I hope with the remarks I wish to receive, there would be more accurate version in the future.

A. A. Abedian K.

Tehran

PREFACE

Proverb Research

Language is a social institution and its most important task is to create links between the communities. Language has long been considered by human as the oldest social phenomenon. Since some centuries B. C., when Panini formulated some rules for Sanskrit language, the complex nature of language became the focus of attention of scholars. This kind of approach gradually led to the emergence of linguistics which systematically examines language as an independent phenomenon. Linguists consider language as the easiest way to convey mental concepts and believe language is the simplest tool that one can use to communicate with others. Sometimes language is referred to as the key of the communication networks, and sometimes as means by which individuals can master it. For the thorough study of language, the intrinsic complexity of language led linguistics to study the descriptive and theoretical aspects of some other disciplines. One of the results of this evolution is the creation of an interdisciplinary domain called Applied Linguistics and a subfield called Paremiology which explores the proverbs. Proverbs are found in all languages, they are considered as part of folklore and social literature. Although proverbs may vary in terms of subjects and functions, it is generally accepted that the majority of the proverbs are adhered to certain social formations. Besides, regardless of the belonging languages, certain syntactic structures are based in the infrastructure of the proverbs. In fact paremiological surveys show that typical traditional examples about the proverbs are: X is Y; No X, no Y; Where there is X, there is Y; and better X than Y.

I

These syntactic structures or proverbial formulae which are in two fundamental affirmative and negative forms are found in Persian and Irish proverbs as well, and are used together with other syntactic markers, phonological markers, and semantic markers as key parts of the proverbs. "From a linguo-cultural perspective, proverbial expressions constitute an important part of the lexicon of a language. Proverbs and other fixed expressions, expressing widely accepted truths, belong to the collective memory of a given language community, shaped over centuries in a given culture"[1].

Studying and surveying nations' culture -especially those who live far apart but still have similarities and common equalities- is one of the most controversial issues in the field of culture. One very important and significant function of the society which its influence on the literature is manifested is proverb; the element that is combined with literature and presented its specific meaning in a literary form and thus have done the style of message transmission beautifully. "Proverbs are short sayings which reflect not only moral conceptions and rules of worldly wisdom, deduced by people from experience and observation, but also reveal traces of culture, nature and theogonic myths, and of historical events. As such, they constitute important ethnological material and command a significant historical value"[2].

---

[1] Serszunowicz (2016).
[2] Champion, 1938: p. 4.

Functions of Proverbs

English anthropologist, Malinowski (1884-1942) in his function oriented theory believes every culture, tradition, object, opinion and belief has a vital function; a task that should be performed and each constitutes an irreplaceable part of the whole organic. He plans the theory of "needs" for explaining practical quality of different culture. In this theory, the function of elements of a culture is satisfying basic human needs. Malinowski borrows his model from natural sciences and recalls that humans constitute as species of animal. The individual feels a number of physiological needs that specify basic requirements. According to the needs theory of Malinowski, it can be concluded that proverbs and their long years of life in the context and reticular of human life is the result of need and continuation of this need during times. That has continued until now and will continue in future as well. One of society needs-to which proverbs respond-is cultural and ethical need in the domain of personal and social issues. This request is concern of gentlefolk and public, because its consequences directly refer to the collective life. Proverbs on one hand flaunt cultural enrichment of a society with their long dating and also themes brought from beyond the millennia; and indicate the ability of thought and speech of predecessors which have seen the world and its events with a careful and critical look and portrayed those issues with an eloquent verbal to the utmost brevity, and on the other hand, having multi-dimensional character and the ability to adapt to different situations in time and space, it has always been reliable and performed its role well in the area of cultural transmission with all its complex dimensions and in other words, duty or function that personal and social education of individuals have burdened on them. Based on Malinowski's theory, the three individual, social and combined functions are conceivable.

Proverbs' Common Functions: Some proverbs have an intermediate state that affects both personal and social life, proverbs refering to Harmful, Punishment of deed, and Seditious and sedition are instances of this type.

Proverbs' Personal Functions: "Although some proverbs condemn those who indulge in sleeping too much: He who sleeps all the morning, may go a-begging all the day after, there are also many proverbial wisdoms connected with the beneficial effects of sleep; take, for example, such proverbs as: Sleep is better than medicine, The beginning of health is sleep, or Sleep is the poor man's treasure. In Norwegian, there is also a well known proverb claiming that if you are asleep, you do not sin: *Den som sover, synder ikke*"[1].

Proverbs' Soicial Functions: "Proverbs are usually seen and defined as the popular expression of some truths learned by life expriences in a linguistic community. They are commonly used in strongly argumentative speeches where the proverb works as an unquestioned truth justified by the experiences of previous generations. The argumentative force of a proverb and its postulate aspect are based on the fact that it is taken as a truth openly proved by experience and therefore it needs no demonstration. However,

---

[1] Abramowicz | Serszunowicz (2016).

paradoxically, the use of a proverb resists that it can be questionable, it can exist another proverb that defends the opposite value and even when it becomes, in some cases, not transparent, when it loses the semantic value it had before and which was justifying its use"[1].

Proverbs and Culture: "History shows that views on the world and on social reality are contextual and depending on cultural values. Proverbial literary heritage have multiple values in establishing a common social meanings or reinterpreting and reconstructing meanings. Proverbs somehow create social identities/collective (for certain), especially when it comes to totalitarian regimes in which their use is significantly amplified"[2].

Proverbs and Literature: "Peoples spread across geographies of affections and memories carrying in their 'traval bag' their dialects, expressions of life, traditions, knowledge and practices. This intangible portion, this spiritual content of the cultural heritage is termed Intangible Cultural Heritage and its identity based in social life and its cultural diversity. Proverbs as well as anecdotes, stories, rhymes, are popular literary expressions that convey wisdom, feelings, beliefs, aspects of everyday life in short, meaningful and logical sentences."[3]

---

[1] Teixeira (2016).
[2] Ylliet | Kapo (2016).
[3] Pereira Da Silva Nunes (2016).

A Brief history of Persian Proverbs

The first Persian proverbs' collection is Rashiduddin vatvat's efforts at the time of Khwarazmshahian in 900 years back. It should be added that Persian has had a considerable (mainly lexical) influence on neighbouring languages, and for centuries, it has been a prestigious cultural language in some regions of Asia by the various empires based in the regions. Following the Turko-Persian Ghaznavid conquest of South Asia, Persian was firstly introduced in the region and afterward it became the official language of the Gurkanian who were ruling India. In this time of the Persian proverbs' history considerable collections like Hablerudi's, Tashkendi's, and Buzrofjei's efforts are done.

In the contemporary era, Allameh Ali Akbar Khan Dehkhodā (1879–1956), a 20th century Paremiologist, Poet, Linguist, Lexicographer, Social Thinker and Political Activist who is best remembered for his Prominent works of Paremiology is counted as the main source for Persian paremiologists. His collection *Amsal O Hekam* was organized into thousands of detailed Asmal (plural of masal means proverb) and Hekam (plural of Hekmat means motto or saying) ranging from general matters to very specific ones. Dehkhodā was born in Tehran, he quickly excelled in Persian literature, Arabic and French and graduated from College studying political science. In 1903, he went to the Balkan Peninsula as an embassy employee, but came back to Iran two years later and became involved in the Constitutional Revolution of Iran. His lexicographic masterpiece *Loghat-Naameh*, is the largest comprehensive Persian dictionary ever published, comprise 16 volumes. The complete work is an ongoing effort that entails over 45 years of efforts by Dehkhodā and a cadre of other experts, up to now 27000 pages of this valuable work is accomplished. In 1925 Iranian law decreed the compilation of an official Persian dictionary, work on the dictionary was begun by Dehkhodā, and upon his death, his residence was named the Dehkhodā Institute and housed the academic staff from several Iranian universities who compiled the dictionary. Afterwards, responsibility for the dictionary was delegated to Tehran University's Department of Persian Language and Literature, and the Dehkhodā Institute became part of University of Tehran. Dehkhodā also annotated Persian literary masterpiece such as classics of Abureyhan Birouni, Naser Khosrow, Seyd Hassan Ghaznavi, Hafez, Manoochehri, Farokhi, Masoud Saed, and Ibn Yamin. He also translated Montesquieu's De l'esprit des lois (The Spirit of the Laws) into Persian, and wrote a French-Persian Dictionary as well. The First World War completely changed the life of Dehkhodā, both as a Paremiologist and a Political Activist and represented a rather general political problem for him, too. The social literary and commentary works of Dehkhodā actually started through his collaboration with Journal of Sur-e Esrafil where he created a satirical political column entitled as *Nonsense* or *Fiddle-Faddle* (*Charand-O-Parand*).

The Persian term of Dakho was his signature or his pen name for that column. Dakho means not only as the Administrator of a Village (Dehkhodā or Kadkhoda), but it also refers to a Naive or an unsophisticated Person who uses proverbs to understand the social phenomenon and to describe his points. Trying to understand why

VII

countries, all through the history misused the society's illiteracy and imposed wars against Iran, he designed this new system of political Naive character, intended to improve social general knowledge and ultimately bring peace. Dehkhodā and his colleague Mirza Jahangir Khan had been publishing the Sur-e Esrafil newspaper for about two years, but the authoritarian King Mohammad-Ali-Shah disbanded the parliament and the media and exiled Dehkhodā and some other liberalists. Dehkhodā continued publishing articles and editorials in exile. Thus, in the end, thoughts about peace and improvement of human affairs led Dehkhodā to his strife to reform the state – an endeavour to which he devoted his life. When King Mohammad-Ali-Shah was deposed in 1911, he returned to the country and became a member of the new Parliament. Dehkhodā's poem (Morghe Sahar) which is called the Persian version of Alfred de Musset's Rappelle-toi, is written in exile in Switzerland's Yverdon-les-Bains about his assassinated colleague Mirza Jahangir Khan Sur-e Esrafil and shows his enthusiasm of peace and brotherhood, his beliefs in principles received national acclaim. Dehkhodā's quest for peace no doubt found its reflection in his lifelong collecting of proverbs.

PERSIAN

&

URDU

Brief History of the Persian Language

Human migration has usually been undertaken to achieve better conditions, as in ancient times, migrations occurred to achieve more water sources and more fertile lands. One of the main events of the second millennium BC [1]was the migration of people with Aryan origins to the Iranian plateau and the Indian-subcontinent. The migration's chronology and land(s) of origin are cited with large differences. In contrast, there are scholars who strongly reject the topic of the Aryans' migration, but historical review of this book is prepared with regard to the common opinion of the Aryans' migration to the Iranian plateau and the Indian-subcontinent. Among the world's languages, the Indo-European language family is the most widespread one. After the migration of people into the Iranian-plateau and the Indian-subcontinent, Indo-European family's language groups were formed, and the group of Iranian languages gradually stemmed out of the Indo-Iranian sub-family. Iranian languages are native to the Iranian Plateau, parts of the Caucasus, and much of Central Asia, which belonged to the Iranian cultural domain until medieval times[2]. With the existence of the Iranian languages' group and the formation of the Persian language, Persian started to improve as one of the main traits of the plateau's inhabitants. Based on historical and structural divisions and from the perspective of language development, linguists assign Iranian languages into three periods: Ancient Era (*First Period*), Medieval Era (*Second Period*), and New Era (*Third Period*).

---

[1] Before the Christian Era.
[2] Borjian, 2015: p. 235.

The distinct development in the transformation of the *Ancient Era* to the *Medieval Era* is changing of the synthetic form of the *Ancient Era* to an analytic form of the *Medieval Era*: nouns, pronouns and adjectives lost their case inflections, prepositions were used to indicate the different roles of words, and many tenses began to be formed from a composite form. The development in the transformation of the *Medieval Era* to the *New Era* were very gradual, and in the 10th–11th centuries Middle Persian texts were still intelligible to speakers of the early phase of the New Persian. However, there are definite differences that had taken place already by the 10th century. Sound changes such as: the dropping of unstressed initial vowels; the epenthesis of vowels in initial consonant clusters; the loss of -g when word finals; and change of initial w- to either b- or (gw- → g-). Changes in the verbal system, notably the loss of distinctive subjunctive and optative forms, and the increasing use of verbal prefixes to express verbal moods. Changes in the vocabulary, particularly the establishment of a superstratum or adstratum of Arabic loanwords replacing many Aramaic loans and native terms, and the substitution of Arabic script for Pahlavi script.

First Period:

The First Period or the *Ancient Era* starts with the existence of the first signs of the Iranian languages and continues up to the late Achaemenid Age. Since the early first millennium BC up to the establishment of the state of the Medes in 708 BC, Iranian languages evolved in different ways and branched into four languages: Scythian, Medes, Avestan, and Old Persian. The writing directions of the Iranian languages in the *Ancient Era* in their earliest forms is written from Right to Left and then -from Left to Right-

Scythian Language: Numerous Scythian tribes over two thousand years —since the first millennium BC— occupied large areas in the eastern and western parts of the Caspian Sea and beyond east and west of the Caspian unto the coast of the Black Sea and the Danube River [1]in the western side and unto the border of China in the eastern side. In inscription of Darius, four Scythian tribes are mentioned; the position of each of the four is one of the states of the Achaemenid Empire. Western Scythians who were called Skothoi by the Greeks had dominated the Median for some time, then the Medes were overpowered and put an end to Scythians' rule. In the times of Scythians and Medes social interaction, their languages effected on each other. Strabo, the Greek geographer of the 1st century CE has noted the languages of the Scythian, the Medes and the Old Persian; and their similarities. From the ethymological point of view, some Scythian words are preserved in areas adjacent to the

---

[1] please see: Reza (2010).

Black Sea; these words, often as particular nouns are remained in Greek and Latin texts. «Some Scythian words as particular nouns are remained in Greek and Latin and Hindi literatures from the Scythians of Central Asia[1]». «There is no remains of the written works from the language of the Scythians or any work that represent the writings of the Scythians[2]»; therefore the direction of the Scythians' writing system cannot be determined.

Medes Language: At the beginning of the first millennium BC, the whole areas of the Amu Darya (Jeyhun) -south of the Aral Sea[3]- and the Sir Darya (Seyhun) rivers were habitations of the Aryans. At this time the Medes and the Pars tribes were located by the Ashur's borders, and their power was gradually rising. In 610 BC, Cyaxares, king of the Medes collaborated with the Babylon's governors and exterminated the Ashur's reign. Herodotus has written that in the time of Diaeco[4], in the early 7th century BC, people's claims' summaries were being written and sent to the Diaeco in his royal court and he would issue the verdict and sent back his judgment to the authorities. Probably the Median government also might issued state documents, but we cannot be certain that these documents have been written in the Medes language. In the first millennium BC, writing system and scribe existed in the territory of Median; but no Median work is inherited to us, and the main source of information about this language are

---

[1] Abolghasemi (2011).
[2] Zarshenas: 1988, p. 557.
[3] the northern part of today Uzbekistan, and the adjacent areas of Turkmenistan and Kazakhstan.
[4] the first king of the Medes.

words and phrases which are used in the inscriptions of the Achaemenid kings who were successors of the Median potentates. It is believed that the Median writing system was in cuneiform scribe, and heretofore all decoded cuneiforms are written from left to right, so likelihood the Medes was written from left to right as well.

Old Persian Language: Old Persian which was the official language of the Achaemenids (6th–4th centuries BC) has close relation with the Sanskrit and the Avestan languages; Old Persian was in use until approximately the 3rd century BC. The official relations of the Achaemenid kings were in Aramaic language and scripts, hence since the Achaemenids quickly overpowered a vast range of areas and they were using the local scribers to manage the affairs of the recessives, therefore besides Old Persian writing system, more inscriptions were incised in other writing systems as well. The Old Persian writing system was used to record important works and it is attested by numerous inscriptions written in cuneiform, most notable of which is the oldest and the most important surviving of them, the great monument of Darius the Great on Mount Behistun, Iran. The inscriptions at Behistun were generally trilingual in Old Persian, Elamite, and Akkadian. After Darius the Great; Xerxes, Artaxerxes I, Darius II, Artaxerxes II, and Artaxerxes III continued the same style. «The alphabet of the Old Persian Language contains 36 letters and 2 word-separators and 8 idiographics. The alphabet had signs as well to represent numbers, but only some of them are inherited to us. Each letter of the alphabet except the three letters which represent the vowels come along with a vowel and because of this the alphabet of the Old Persian is syllabic. The Old Persian alphabet was written from left to right, this alphabet were being used up to the end of the Achaemenids kingdom, but later it became obsolesced and later reading of the Old Persian alphabet was forgotten[1]».

Avestan Language: Avestan was the language of one of the regions in East Iran in the *Ancient Era*. Avestan writing system known as *Din-e-Dabireh* was created with derivation of the Pahlavi writing system in the 3rd century CE, during the Sasanid Age. From the Avestan writing system except the religious book of the Zoroastrian religion, *Avesta*, nothing else is discovered, yet. The phonetic alphabet of the Avestan is a clear and simple writing system, scribing from right to left in separate form, and everywhere its characters come, they have the same form. Avestan writing system has 42 letters and is more complete than the Pahlavi's. In writing the phonemes, Avestan is more complete than today's (*Modern*) Persian writing system; and to script phonemes like *KH*, *CH*, *GH*, and *SH* in English language or *SCH* in German language, the Avestan writing system does not need to accumulate different characters.

---

[1] Abolghasemi (2011).

Second Period:

The Second Period or the *Medieval Era* starts with the collapse of the Achaemenids and the establishment of the Greco Seleucids monarchy, and continues with the Parthians and Sasanids and the first centuries after Arab invasions. The *Medieval Era* has two main categories: Sakan, Sogdian, Chorasmian, and Bactarian in its Eastern Category; and Arsacid, and Middle Persian in its Wastern Category. These names are given to middle stage of development of the numerous Iranian languages and dialects[1].

Eastern Category: This category includes Sakan, Sogdian, Chorasmian, and Bactarian languages. It is thought languages of the Eastern Category have been separated from Western Iranian languages in the course of the later 2nd millennium BC. With the Greeks invasion and their presence in Central Asia, some of the languages of this category moved towards easternmost.

Sakan Language: Sakan [2]is an Iranian language of the *Medieval Era* in its Eastern Category and it is attested from the ancient kingdoms of Khotan and Tumshuq in the Tarim Basin[3].
The two dialects of Khotanese and Tumshuqese are formed due to the movement of the Scythians. It is believed that the Tarim Basin became linguistically Turkified by the end of the 11th century[4]. No invasion of

---

[1] Henning (1958).
[2] sometimes called Khotanese-Saka and Scytho-Khotanese.
[3] in what is now Southern Xinjiang, China.
[4] Akiner, 2013: p. 71.

the region is recorded in Chinese records and one theory is that two tribes of the Saka (Khotan and Tumshuq), settled in the region in about 200 BC before the Chinese accounts commence[1]. No direct evidence has been found to relate the Sakan (of the *Medieval Era*) to the Scythian Language (of the *Ancient Era*) as an earlier version of the language[2].

Other than an inscription from Issyk Kurgan that it is tentatively identified as Khotanese (although written in Kharosthi), all of the surviving documents originate from Khotan or Tumshuq. The earliest texts, from the 4th century, are mostly religious documents. Many of them are reports (called haṣda aurāsa) to the royal court which are of historical importance, as well as private documents. Discovered documents date from the 4th to the 11th century. Tumshuqese was more archaic than Khotanese, but it is much less understood because it appears in fewer manuscripts compared to Khotanese[3]. The language was known as *Hvatanai* in contemporary documents[4]. In the 11th century, it was remarked by Mahmud al-Kashgari that the people of Khotan still have their own language and script and did not know Turkic well[5].

Sogdian Language: Sogdian is an Iranian language of the *Medieval Era* in its Eastern Category. Sogdian is usually assigned to a Northeastern group of the Iranian languages. No direct evidence of an earlier version of the

---

[1] Bailey (1970).
[2] although rarely called Medieval Scythia.
[3] Masson, 1992; p. 283.
[4] Bailey (1939).
[5] Scott | Sela, 2010: p. 72.

language in *Ancient Era* has been found, although mention of Sogdia in the inscriptions of the Old Persian shows that a separate and recognisable area existed at least since the Achaemenid Empire. The Sogdian as an Eastern language of the *Medieval Era* like Khotanese, possesses   conservative grammar and morphology more than the Western languages of the *Medieval Era* like Middle Persian. During Tang Empire by the Sui dynasty of China (7th century CE), Sogdian became the *lingua franca* of the Silk Road and the economic level of Sogdia increased; and its economic and political importance guaranteed its survival in the first few centuries after the Muslim conquest of Sogdia in the early 8th century[1]. Like all the writing systems employed for the Iranian languages of the *Medieval Era*, the Sogdian alphabet ultimately derives from the Aramaic alphabet. As in other writing systems descended from the Proto-Sinaitic script, there are no special signs for vowels. However the consonant signs would also sometimes serve to express the short vowels, which could sometimes be left unexpressed, as they always are in the parent systems[2]. To distinguish long vowels from short ones, an additional *aleph* could be written before the sign denoting the long vowel[3].

The Sogdian also used the Manichaean alphabet, which consisted of 29 letters[4]. Sogdian scripts like Pahlavi,

---

[1] a dialect of Sogdian spoken around the 8th century near Istaravshan in Tajikistan, developed into Yaghnobi and has survived into this century (Bergne, 2007: p. 6).

[2] in the parent Aramaic system, the consonantal signs ' y w can be used as matres lectionis for the long vowels [a: i: u:].

[3] Clauson, 2002: pp. 103-104.

[4] Gershevitch (1954).

contains many logograms or ideograms, which were Aramaic words written to represent native spoken ones.

Chorasmian Language: Chorasmian is an Iranian language of the *Medieval Era* in its Eastern Category, and it is closely related to Sogdian. Knowledge of Chorasmian is limited to the *Medieval Era* and, as with Sogdian, little is known of its *Ancient Era*. The Chorasmian language was spoken in the area of Chorasmia[1], centered in the lower Amu Darya (Jeyhun), south of the Aral Sea. Rather than this Chorasmian, an older type (Old Chorasmian) can be estimated which developed into the newer version. Old Chorasmian was written in an indigenous script descended from the Aramaic, brought to the region by the administration of the Achaemenid Empire and characterized by heterography, that is, the occasional writing of Aramaic words to represent the corresponding Chorasmian. It is known earliest from coin inscriptions and documents on wood and parchment from about the end of the 2nd century CE, and latest from inscriptions on some silver vessels but mainly from ossuary inscriptions of the late 7th century. The paucity of this material, however, and its fragmentary nature do not allow an analysis of the language[2]. Before the advance of Islam in Chorasmia in the early 8th century, Chorasmian was written in a script close to that of Sogdian and Pahlavi with its roots in the Imperial Aramaic script.
From the few surviving examples of this script on coins and artifacts it has been observed that written

---

[1] Khwarezm.
[2] MacKenzie, 1991: pp. 517-520.

Chorasmian included Aramaic logograms or ideograms[1]. After the advance of Islam, Chorasmian was written using a n adapted version of the Perso-Arabic alphabet with a few extra signs to reflect specific Chorasmian sounds, such as the letter څ, which represents /ts/ and /dz/, as in the traditional Pashto orthography[2]. This modified script, is attested from the 5th to 8th centuries, by which time the language was evidently well on the way to disuse, having been Turkified. The earliest examples have been left by the Chorasmian scholar Abū Rayḥān Bīrūnī, in his works on chronology and astronomy, he recorded calendrical and astronomical terms, some of the traditional names of days, months, feasts, and signs of the zodiac. By far the greater part of the Chorasmian vocabulary preserved for us is to be found in the form of interlinear glosses throughout a single manuscript of the celebrated Arabic dictionary *Moqaddamat-al-adab* by another native Chorasmian, Zamakšarī.

In contrast to these monotonous dictionary entries, other Chorasmian texts include the 400 odd whole or partial sentences quoted, to illustrate case law, in a series of Arabic law books emanating from Chorasmia: the *Yatīmat-al-dahr* by Alā-al-Dīn Tarjomānī, the *Monyat-al-foqahā* by Faḵr-al-Dīn Qobaznī, and an augmented résumé of the latter, the *Qonyat-al-monya*, by Moḵtār Zāhedī Ḡazmīnī.

---

[1] Aramaic words written to represent native spoken ones.
[2] MacKenzie (1991).

Bactarian Language: Bactarian[1] is an Iranian language of the *Medieval Era* in its Eastern Category, this language shares features with Sogdian and Chorasmian of the *Medieval Era*[2]. Its genealogical position is unclear[3]. Bactrian which was used as the official language of the Kushan and the Hephthalite dynasties was spoken in the Central Asian region of Bactria[4]. Under Kushan rule, Bactria became known as *Tukhara* or *Tokhara*, and later as *Tokharistan*, as well as sometimes *Eteo-Tocharian* (i.e. *true* or *original Tocharian*)[5]. Following the conquest of Bactria by Alexander in 323 BC, and the establishment of Hellenistic there, for about two centuries Greek was the administrative language of the Seleucid and the Greco-Bactrian.

By the fall of the Seleucids in Iran and the decreasing of the Greeks power, the Eastern Scythian tribes of the Saka invaded the territory around 140 BC, and at some time after 124 BC, Bactria was overrun by a confederation of tribes belonging to the Great Yuezhi and Tokhari. In the 1st century CE, the Kushana (one of the Yuezhi tribes)

---

[1] Bactrian or Greco-Bactrian, Kushano-Bactrian or Kushan.

[2] Bactrian shares features with the Pashto, Yidgha, and Munji (of the Eastern Category), as well as with the Arsacid Pahlavi (of the Western Category); please see: Henning, 1960: p. 47.

[3] Novák, 2014: pp. 77–87.

[4] or Balḵ; present-day Afghanistan and Tajikistan.

[5] in early 20th century, two extinct Indo-European languages were discovered in the Tarim Basin, they were linked circumstantially to Tokharistan, and Bactrian was sometimes referred to as "Eteo-Tocharian". By the 1970s, it was clear that there is little evidence for such connection, i.e. the Tarim *Tocharian* languages were part of the *centum group* and were most closely related to the Anatolian languages, whereas Bactrian was a *satemised* Iranian language.

founded the ruling dynasty of the Kushan, initially the Kushana retained the Greek language for administrative purposes, but soon began to use Bactrian; the Greek script however remained and was used to write Bactrian. In using Greek alphabet, ambiguities remain, some of the disadvantages were overcome by using heta (Ⱶ, ⱶ) for /h/ and by introducing sho (Ϸ, ϸ) to represent /ʃ/. *Xi* (Ξ, ξ) and *psi* (Ψ, ψ) were not used to write Bactrian, as the *ks* and *ps* sequences do not occur in Bactrian. They were however probably used to represent numbers and other Greek letters. In the 3rd century, the Kushan territories in the west of the Indus river fell to the Sasanids, and Bactrian began to be influenced by the Middle Persian. Next to Pahlavi script and (occasionally) Brahmi script, some coinage of this period is still in Greco-Bactrian script. Beginning in the mid-4th century, Bactria and Northwestern India yielded to the Hephthalite tribes.

The Hephthalite period is marked by linguistic diversity and in addition to Bactrian, Middle Persian, North Indo-Aryan, Turkish and Latin vocabulary is also attested. The Hephthalites ruled their territories until the 7th century when they were overrun by the Arabs, after which the official use of Bactrian ceased. Although Bactrian briefly survived in other usage, that too eventually ceased, and the latest examples of the language date to the end of the 9th century[1]. The present-day speakers of Munji, the modern Eastern Iranian language of the Munjan Valley in Northeast Afghanistan, display the closest possible linguistic affinity with the Bactrian language[2].

---

[1] Harmatta, 1994: p. 433.
[2] Waghmar, 2001: pp. 40–48.

Knowledge of Bactarian is limited to the *Medieval Era* and little is known of its *Ancient Era*; although it was long thought that *Avestan* (of the *Ancient Era*) represented *Old Bactrian*, but this notion had "rightly fallen into discredit by the end of the 19th century"[1].

---

[1] Gershevitch, 1983: p. 1250.

Western Category: This category includes Arsacid and Middle Persian languages. The Westen Category is a branch of the Iranian languages, attested from the time of Old Persian (6th century BC) and the Median languages.

Arsacid Language: Arsacid[1] is an Iranian language of the *Medieval Era* in its Western Category. Nothing has been found of the ancient form of the Arsacid language. The Parthian Arsacids called their language Parthawik meaning Parthian[2], via regular sound changes Parthawik became Pahlawik, from which the word *Pahlavi* eventually evolved. Arsacid was the language of the old Satrapy of Parthia[3], and was used in the Arsacids courts. Following the overthrow of the Seleucids in the 3rd century BC, the Parthian Arsacids adopted the manner, customs and government of the court of two centuries previously[4]. When Parthians established their dynasty, Arsacid gradually became the language of state of the Arsacid Parthian Empire (248 BC–224 CE), as well as of its eponymous branches of the Arsacid dynasty of Armenia, the Arsacid dynasty of

---

[1] Arsacid or Arsacid Pahlavi, Parthian, Parthian Pahlavi, Pahlavani, and Pahlawānīg.
It is also called Chaldeo-Pahlavi, or Northwest Pahlavi, the latter reflecting its apparent development from a dialect that was almost identical to that of the Medes. Kent (1950).

[2] in the Medieval Era *ik* was a regular appurtenant suffix for "pertaining to", *-ik* is still in use in Tabari; in New Persian *-ik* is shortened to *-i*.

[3] a region lies along the Southern/Southeastern edge of the Caspian sea, it is adjacent to the boundary between Western and Eastern Iranian languages.

[4] they considered themselves the legitimate heirs of the Achaemenids.

Iberia, and the Arsacid dynasty of Caucasian Albania. Contact with other languages made Arsacid share some features of the Eastern Iranian language group, the influence of which is attested primarily in loanwords. Some traces of Eastern influence survive in Arsacid loanwords in Armenian[1]. It is also believed that *Tabari* language can be regarded as the lineage of Arsacid. When the Arsacids came to power, under the cultural influence of the Greeks (Hellenization), they inherited the use of written Greek as the writing system of their dynasty. But yet other languages of the *Medieval Era* began to be written in a script derived from Aramaic, as it had previously been the writing system of the former Achaemenids. This practice had led to others adopting Imperial Aramaic as the language of communications, both between Iranians and non-Iranians, as well as among Iranians[2]. The transition from Imperial Aramaic took place very slowly, with a slow increase of more and more Iranian words so that Aramaic with Iranian elements gradually changed into Iranian with Aramaic elements. Under Arsacid hegemony, this Aramaic-derived writing system came to be associated with the Parthians in particular (it may have originated in the Parthian chancellories[3]), and thus the writing system came to be called Pahlavi (Parthian) too[4]. The use of Pahlavi gained popularity following its adoption as the language/script of the commentaries

---

[1] a large part of Armenian vocabulary was formed primarily by borrowings from Arsacid; now many Arsacid words can be traced in Armenian; please see: Lecoq (1983).

[2] Gershevitch (1983).

[3] Boyce (1983).

[4] Boyce (1968).

(Zend) on the *Avesta*[1]. Propagated by the priesthood, who were not only considered to be transmitters of all knowledge but were also instrumental in government, the use of Pahlavi eventually reached all corners of the Parthian Arsacid Empire. Arsacid used Pahlavi writing system with two essential characteristics: first, its script derived from Aramaic (the script and language of the Achaemenid chancellery, i.e. Imperial Aramaic)[2]; second, it had a high incidence of Aramaic words, rendered as ideograms or logograms[3]. Arsacid was used until about the 4th century or the 6th century CE. The most ancient works in the Arsacid language date back to 100 BC. Works written in the Arsacid can be divided into two categories: works in Arsacid handwriting, and works written in the Manichaean scripts based on a type of Aramaic writing system. Arsacid handwriting was written from right to left and the characters are not joined to each other. The main characteristic of this handwriting is the presence of writing elements called *Hezvarash*, the *words* that are written in the Arsacid, but in reading, their equivalent words (another word which has the same meaning) are read. For instance, the word *Molka* which has the same meaning as *Shah* (King) is read as *Shah* because its equivalent in the Arsacid is *Shah*. The latest works in Arsacid are Manichaean works which were generally written before the 9th century CE. These works were written at a time when the Arsacid was no longer used. The Manichaean texts were written in

---

[1] Mirza, 2002. pp. 162–163.

[2] among the many practices so adopted by the Arsacids from the Achaemenids, was the use of the Imperial Aramaic that together with Aramaic script served as the language of the chancellery.

[3] they were written Aramaic words but understood as Arsacid.

Arsacid even until the 13th century CE. In fact, after the spread of the Manichaean religion in Khorasan and Chorasmia with the efforts of Manichaean missionaries, the Arsacid was used as a tool for promoting the Manichaean religion and hence books were written or translated in this language. The handwriting used for these texts is the same as the Manichaean handwriting said to be invented based on a type of Aramaic handwriting by Mani himself. The Manichaean handwriting direction is from right to left and its main characteristic is lack of *Hezvarash* which makes this writing very easy to read. Also unlike the Arsacid writing system in which each letter can have different phonetic values, in Manichaean writing system each letter can only have one phonetic value. There are two books written in Middle Persian in which Arsacid words are determinable. Experts estimate these books were originally versified and were written in Arsacid, the two books are: *Yadegar-e-zariran*, and *Derakht-e-asuri*[1]. Most probably, the Persian poem of *Vis-o-Ramin* written by Fakhr Al-Din Asad Gorgani has Arsacid roots, some love stories of *Šāh-nāma* (i.e. Bijan and Manijeh) might be Arsacid legends, as well.

Middle Persian Language: Middle Persian [2]is an Iranian language of the *Medieval Era* in its Western Category. Middle Persian (of the *Medieval Era*) descends from the Old Persian (of the *Ancient Era*) and is the linguistic ancestor of the Modern Persian (of the *New*

---

[1] Asouri Tree; it is a discussion between a tree and a goat to see which one is more useful for human being.

[2] Middle Persian or Sasanian Pahlavi, Sasanid Pahlavi, Persian Pahlavi, Southwest Pahlavi, Pahlavi, and Parsik.

Era). Following the defeat of the Arsacids by the Sasanids, the latter inherited the Empire and its institutions, and with it, the use of the Aramaic-derived language and its writing system. Middle Persian gradually became a prestige dialect and so came to be spoken in other regions of the Empire from the 3rd century BC to the 9th century CE. Like the Arsacids before him, Ardeshir, the founder of the Sasanids (3rd-7th centuries CE)[1], projected himself as a successor to the royal traditions of the Achaemenids, in particular those of Artaxerxes II, whose throne name the new emperor adopted. The Sasanids had inherited the bureaucracy, and the affairs of government went on as Arsacids, with the use of dictionaries such as the *Frahang-i-Pahlavig* assisting the transition; therefore from a linguistic point of view, there was probably little disruption. Arsacid language did not die out with the Arsacids, and is represented in some bilingual inscriptions alongside the Middle Persian; by the parchment manuscripts of Auroman; and by certain Manichaean texts from Turpan. Furthermore, the archaic orthography of Middle Persian continued to reflect, in many respects, pronunciations that had been used in Arsacid times. Ardeshir himself came from a clergy tradition, and as such would have been proficient in the language and script. Moreover, both languages of Arsacids and Middle Persian belong to the Western Category of the *Medieval Era*, hence, Arsacids was closely related to the dialect of the southwest[2]. Middle Persian

---

[1] Borjian, 2015: p. 236.

[2] which was more properly called Pārsi, that is, the language of Pārsā, Persia proper; please see: Boyce (2002).

was written in modified Aramaic scripts and is represented by numerous epigraphic texts of Sasanids kings. There is also a varied literature in Middle Persian embracing both the Manichaean and the Zoroastrian religious traditions, which are known as Manichaean-Middle-Persian and Zoroastrian-Middle-Persian. Traces of Middle Persian are found in remnants of Sasanian inscriptions and Egyptian papyri, coins and seals, fragments of Manichaean writings[1], and treatises and Zoroastrian books from the Sasanian Era, as well as in the post-Sasanian Zoroastrian variant of the language sometimes known as Pahlavi, that originally referred to the Pahlavi scripts[2], which was also the preferred writing system for several other languages of the *Medieval Era*, aside from the Aramaic alphabet-derived script[3].

---

[1] Manichaean texts were written in the Manichaean alphabet derives from a type of Aramaic alphabetys, but in an Eastern category of the Medieval Era form via the Sogdian alphabet.

[2] Zoroastrian-Middle-Persian was occasionally also written in Pazend, a system derived from the Avestan alphabet that, unlike Pahlavi, indicated vowels and did not employ logograms.

[3] Spooner, 2012: p. 14.

Third Period:

The Third Period or the *New Era* starts with the establishment of the first Persian governments after the Arab invasion. Symbolically it is said the *New Era* starts since the Saffarids first king rejected the use of Arabic.

In the *Third Period*, Middle Persian developed into New Persian which is in use since then, today as Modern Persian. In the 7th century, the Sasanids were overthrown by the Arab invasion. Under Arab influence, Iranian languages began to be written in Arabic script (adapted to their phonology accordingly), while Middle Persian began to rapidly evolve into New Persian and its name became Arabicized as *Farsi*. All Iranians were not comfortable with these Arabic-influenced developments, in particular, members of the literate elite, which in Sasanid times consisted primarily of Zoroastrian priests. Those former elites continued to use the *old* language (i.e. Middle Persian) and Aramaic-derived writing system[1]. In time, the name of the writing system, Pahlavi (Parthian), began to be applied to the *old* Middle Persian language as well, thus distinguishing it from the *new* language, *Farsi*[2]. As almost all discovered Middle Persian literature is in this particular late form of exclusively written Zoroastrian-Middle-Persian, the term *Pahlavi* became synonymous with Middle Persian itself. Pahlavi is the language of quite a large body of literature which details the traditions and prescriptions of Zoroastrianism, which was the state religion of Sasanian Iran.

The earliest texts in Zoroastrian-Middle-Persian were

---

[1] Boyce, 1968: p. 33.
[2] Boyce, 1968: pp. 32-33.

probably written down in late Sasanian times (6th–7th centuries), although they represent the codification of earlier oral tradition[1]. However, most texts, including the translated versions of the Zoroastrian canon, date from the 9th to 11th centuries, when Middle Persian had long ceased to be a spoken language, so they reflect the state of affairs in living Middle Persian only indirectly. There are texts of the Judeo-Middle-Persian [2]varieties too; but less abundantly attested varieties are Manichaean-Middle-Persian used for a sizable amount of Manichaean religious writings, including many theological texts, homilies and hymns; and Christian-Middle-Persian as the Middle Persian of the Church of the East, evidenced in the Pahlavi Psalter (7th century). These were used until the beginning of the second millennium in many places in Central Asia, including Turpan and even localities in South India. All three differ minimally from one another and indeed the less ambiguous and archaizing scripts of the latter two have helped to elucidate some aspects of the Sasanian-Era pronunciation of the former[3]. In view of some linguistic features such as lexical scope, and so on, Persian is one of the richest languages of the *Third Period*; hence, there are other languages which belong to this Era, the most four important of them are Kurdish, Baluchi, Pashto, Ossetian and Tabari.

---

[1] Sundermann, 1989: p. 141.

[2] The term Judeo-Persian is coined by Western scholars to designate the Persian language when written in Hebrew script. (Borjian, 2015: pp. 235-236-239).

[3] Sundermann, 1989: pp. 138-143.

Kurdish Language: Kurdish belongs to the Western Iranian group of the Indo-Iranian branch of the Indo-European family, spoken in three dialect groups known as Kurmanji, Sorani, and Palewani[1]. Windfuhr (2009) notes although Kurdish languages are generally classified as Northwestern Iranian languages, some scholars classify them as an intermediate between Northwestern and Southwestern Iranian languages. Windfuhr (1975) and Frye (1984) assume an eastern origin for Kurdish and consider it as related to eastern and central Iranian dialects[2]. Paul (2008) concludes that Kurdish seems to be a Northwestern Iranian language in origin, but acknowledges that it shares many traits with Southwestern Iranian languages like Persian, apparently due to longstanding and intense historical contacts. A separate group of the Zaza–Gorani languages, are also spoken by Kurds. Gorani is classified as part of the Zaza–Gorani branch of Indo-Iranian languages[3]. Some scholars divide Zaza-Gorani in complete separated groups. Haig|Öpengin (2015) in their study suggest grouping the Kurdish languages into Northern Kurdish, Central Kurdish, Southern Kurdish, Zaza, and Gorani, and avoid the subgrouping Zaza–Gorani[4].

Kurmanji and Sorani are two principal branches of Kurdish, Kurmanji is the language of the vast majority of Kurds in Turkey, Syria, Armenia, Azerbaijan, and of a few in Iraq and Iran, the area designated by Kurdish nationalists as North Kurdistan (Kurdistana Bakûr); and

---

[1] Kreyenbroek (1992).

[2] Windfuhr, 1975: pp. 457-471. Frye, 1984: p. 29.

[3] Postgate, 2007: p. 138.

[4] For more information, please refer to: Abd al-Jabbar (2008).

Sorani, the language of most Kurds in Iraq and Iran, the area designated as South Kurdistan (Kurdistana Başûr) by this nationalist classifiers. Although the two languages are closely related, Kurmanji and Sorani are not mutually intelligible and differ at the basic structural level as well as in the vocabulary. The line dividing Kurmanji from Sorani runs roughly diagonally from northeast to southwest. The extreme northwest of Iran and the northernmost tip of Iraq fall into the Kurmanji-speaking area[1]. In historical evolution terms, Kurmanji is less modified than Sorani and Pehlewani in both phonetic and morphological structure. The Sorani group has been influenced by, among other things, its closer cultural proximity to the other languages spoken by Kurds in the region including the Gorani language in parts of Iranian Kurdistan and Iraqi Kurdistan[2].

Baluchi Language[3]: Baluchi is the principal language of the Baluch spoken in Iran, Pakistan and Afghanistan. Baluchi is a member of the Western Iranian group of languages, bearing affinities to both main representatives of Western Middle Iranian languages: Middle Persian and Parthian. Baluchi has, however, a marked individuality of its own, and differs from both of these languages in important respects. Baluchi is in all essentials a Northwestern Iranian language, closely related to the Middle Iranian Parthian and modern Kurdish, Tāti, Tāleši, and other dialects[4]. Six major dialects can be distinguished for Baluchi, differing from

---

[1] Thackston (2006).
[2] Kreyenbroek (1992).
[3] main source: Elfenbein (1988).
[4] please see: MacKenzie (1961).

each other in phonology, morphology, syntax, and lexicon. Of these, Rakšāni is by far the most widely spoken, and can itself be subdivided into three regional varieties. The other five dialects are fairly uniform. It is important to realize that Baluchi is a conservative language, and its dialects, in spite of the vastness of the area in which they are spoken, are quite remarkably similar; with the exception of Eastern Hill Baluchi, speakers from all areas readily understand one another. Proceeding roughly from north to south the dialects are: Rakšāni, Sarāvāni, Lāšāri, Kechi, Coastal dialects, and Eastern Hill Baluchi. Baluchi Phonology has a simple phonemic structure: the vowels are: $a, i, u, \bar{a}, \bar{\imath}, \bar{u}, \bar{e}, \bar{o}$; with diphthongs ay, aw.

The consonants are: $p, t, k, b, d, g, ṭ, ḍ$ (stops); $č, j$ (affricates); $s, z, š$, (sibilants); $w, y, l, m, n, r, ṛ, ṇ$ (continuants). The spirants f, x, γ are common in loanwords in all dialects, but tend rapidly to p, k, g respectively as the words become naturalized. Eastern Hill Baluchi, uniquely, keeps them, and in addition has also developed θ and $'$ from postvocalic t and d; and intervocalic b tends to become v.

Morphologycally, Baluchi, like most Western Iranian languages has lost the Old Iranian gender distinctions. Its commonest ending for the oblique plural of nouns is -$\bar{a}n$, which is the characteristic of Western Iranian languages. Similarly, the originally collective suffix -gal, now used as a plural suffix is found in Kurdish, Fārs dialects, and some Central dialects. Baluchi syntax shows that the *eżāfa* construction characteristic of Persian and other (South)-western Iranian languages, including Kurdish, is not used in Baluchi, except occasionally (as in most modern Iranian languages) in some types of formal poetry and in stereotyped phrases borrowed from Persian. Characteristic of most Baluchi dialects except Rak̲šāni is the common Iranian passive (also called ergative) construction of past transitive verbs. Rak̲šāni is the only dialect to have adopted the active construction, probably from Persian. North Rak̲šāni is the only dialect to use exclusively the active construction; Central and Southern Rak̲šāni (and all other dialects) use *ergative* constructions, either partly or entirely. The normal word order is subject–object–verb. Like many other Indo-Iranian languages, Baluchi also features split ergativity. The subject is marked as nominative except for the past tense constructions where the subject of a transitive verb is marked as oblique and the verb agrees with the object. On the whole, however, the linguistic position of Baluchi is obscured by its numerous borrowings, principally lexical (though there are some syntactic ones as well); there are also certainly substrate influences from languages spoken in areas in which Baluch have dwelt for long periods during their migrations, or with whom they have had close contact. All Baluchi dialects possess numerous loanwords from several different Indo-Aryan languages, which may be the result of independent Baluch migrations at different times.

Pashto Language[1]: Pashto is spoken in South and Southeastern Afghanistan, by recent settlers in Northern Afghanistan, in Pakistan (North-West Frontier Province and Baluchistan), and on the eastern border of Iran. After Persian, Pashto is the second in importance among the

---

[1] main source: Morgenstierne (1982).

Iranic languages of the *New Era*. Pashto undoubtedly belongs to the Northeastern Iranic branch. As regards the one possible exception, Waṇecī which is the only dialect that stands decidedly apart, spoken in Northeast Baluchistan between Harnai and Loralai, and now being more and more influenced by and pushed back by ordinary Pashto. It is possible that the original home of Pashto may have been in Badakšān with some contact with a Saka dialect akin to Khotanese. But it seems that the Old Iranic ancestor dialect of Pashto must have been close to that of the Gathas. It is important to note that the early and profound influence of Indo-Aryan on Pashto as well as Pashto's remarkable preservation of many Iranic morphological features, in which respect only Ossetian can compete with or even surpass it. There appear to be no special agreements between Pashto and any Pamir languages, whether in phonology, morphology, or vocabulary. Although there are numerous different dialects, Pashto is essentially one language[1]. Due to overlaps among various isoglosses, it is difficult to establish a satisfactory classification of Pashto dialects. Thus the dialects presenting a further development of common Pashto vocalism may belong either to the "soft" or the "hard" group. Nor are the results of palatalization, metathesis, etc., confined to definitive areas. It may therefore be practical to deal with the dialect features in connection with the description of phonemic and morphological development. Pashto shares with Munjī the change of $*\delta > l$, but this tendency extends also to Sogdian. The Waṇecī dialect shares with Munjī the change of *-t-* > *-y-*/o. If we assume that this

---

[1] please see: Morgenstierne (1930).

agreement points to some special connection, and not to a secondary, parallel development, we should have to admit that one branch of pre-Pashto had already, before the splitting off of Waṇecī, retained some special connection with Munjī, an assumption unsupported by any other facts. Pashto has *dr-, wr-* < **θr-*, **fr*-like Khotanese Saka. Although to a large extent the native elements of the Pashto vocabulary are related to the vocabularies of other Iranic languages, a remarkably large number of words is special to Pashto[1]. Changes in the Pashto's phonemic system is similar to the Persian's changes. According to the orthography of "classical" Pashto recorded since the 10ᵗʰ-16ᵗʰ centuries, there were 31 consonants, including *q*, *f* [2]and *ayn*. Arabic *ṭ*, is pronounced as *t, t̲* and *ṣ* as *s*, and *d̲, ż*, and *z̤* as *z*. Retroflex *ṭ*, and *ḍ* are restricted to loanwords from Indo-Aryan vocabulary, but a large number of these are of ancient date and no more felt as foreign. The remaining 26 consonants occur in words of genuine Pashto origins, except *h* which is rare in original words:*k, g, γ; t, d, n; p, b, m; ṇ; č, ǰ; c, j; s, š, x; z, ž, ǧ; r, ṛ, l; y, w, h.* The vowels are: *a, i, u,* ə *(zwarg'ay); ā, ī, ū, ē,* and *ō.* The vowels *a* and ə overlap in some dialects and *ī* and *ū* have been abbreviated in most of them. For standard Pashto *ē* and *ō* will be written *e* and *o*, since there is no opposition between long and short *e* and *o* (except in the cases where *i* may be pronounced as short *e*). Diphthongs are *āy, āw*, and final *-əy*. Characteristic of Pashto is the role played by mobile stress.

---

[1] for details please see: Morgenstierne (1927).
[2] only in loanwords and largely pronounced as *k* and *p*.

Ossetian Language[1]: Ossetian (Ossetic) is an Iranian language spoken in the Central Caucasus, mainly in the North Ossetian Republic (Alaniya) of the Russian Federation and in the South Ossetian [2]area of Georgia. In addition, minor Ossetian settlements exist at various places in the North Caucasus. An Ossetian-speaking population is also found in a few villages in central and eastern Anatolia (Turkey), the descendants of refugees who left their native country in the North Caucasus in the 1860s; there is a minor Ossetian-speaking population in Hungary too. Ossetian belongs to the eastern branch of the Iranian languages. The linguistic ancestors of the present-day Ossetes were Alan tribes [3]who, according to Greek and Roman sources, emigrated from Central Asia to the lands north and east of the Black Sea about the beginning of the Christian Era. The Alans were, in their heyday in the early Middle Ages, a predominant people in the Northwest Caucasus, and their dialects were widespread in the area. The language was gradually ousted by Turkic and Cherkes immigrants from the west and north, and it is now limited to a relatively small region. There is some evidence that the present Ossetian-speaking area was formerly inhabited by Nakh-speaking

---

[1] main source: Thordarson (2009).

[2] until 1990, autonomous.

[3] Alans, an ancient Iranian tribe of the northern (Scythian, Saka, Sarmatian, Massagete) group, known to classical writers from the first centuries AD. Their name appears in Greek as Alanoi, in Latin as Alani or Halani. The same tribes, or affiliated ones, are mentioned as the Asaioi (by Ptolemy), Rhoxolanoi, Aorsoi, Sirakoi, and Iazyges (by Strabo). In early times the main mass of the Alans was settled north of the Caspian and Black seas. Later they also occupied the Crimea and considerable territory in the Northern Caucasus.

(Ingush-Chechen, the Northeast Caucasus) tribes. The previous presence of the Alans in the Northwest Caucasus is borne out by a number of place names of Iranian origin in modern Turkish and Cherkes areas. Ossetian, like its Alanic predecessor, has for millennia been separated from the sister languages of Central Asia, being spoken in non-Iranian surroundings. It has developed certain characteristic peculiarities, in part due to the influence of adjacent languages (Turkic, Caucasic)[1]. This applies to vocabulary as well as phonetic and grammatical structure. As regards lexical borrowing, the influence of Turkic languages seems to have been particularly strong. In general, however, the Ossetian grammatical structure has been resistant to foreign influence. Especially the verb has roughly retained the character of Old Aryan. The verb is unipersonal, showing concord with only one actant of the clause. Ergativity, which is traditionally considered as common to the Caucasic languages, has not penetrated Ossetian, either syntactically or morphologically. The subject of the verb is almost invariably put in the nominative. Actually, Ossetian has gone through a stage of ergativity: the genitive continues to be used as the subject of the past tense of transitive verbs. This historical stage is also still reflected in the use of the genitive case of the personal

---

[1] like the voiceless unaspirated glottalic stops, that is, stops accompanied by a closure of the vocal cords: p', t', c', č', k' (q'). Unlike the Caucasic languages, the functional load of the glottalization is inessential in Ossetic; minimal pairs opposing t' and t, d, etc. are rare. In loanwords, the Russian voiceless stops and affricates are usually rendered by their glottalic counterparts, even if this practice is not shown by the orthography.

pronoun of the 1st and 2nd plural as the subject case. Like most other modern Iranian languages, Ossetian has abandoned the ergative system. Ossetian falls into two distinct dialects which are barely mutually intelligible: Iron [1] and Digor[2]. There is some variation within each dialect; the idiom of the South Ossetes is a variant of Iron. The literary and administrative language is based on Iron. In all essentials Digor represents a more archaic stage of development; the relationship of the dialects can be described in the terms of a focal versus a marginal dialect. The basic core of the lexicon, words signifying elementary human experience, are mostly of Iranian languages origin. Turkish and Caucasic loanwords are, as a rule, denotations of social and natural phenomena peculiar to the Caucasus. It is noteworthy that quite a large number of plant names seem to be of Turkish origin. So far three medieval Alanic texts have been identified[3]; in addition there exist two short lists of words from the 17th-18th centuries [4]and a few texts with a list of words and a short grammatical sketch. Phonologically, in principle Old Iranian final *ă, short and long *i* and *u* have been lost. Initial and medial *ă (hă) becomes *ä* in both dialects of Iron and Digor, unless there follow two consonants. If there is a morpheme boundary between the two consonants, *ă (hă) becomes *ä*, *ă (hă) also becomes *ä* if it is followed by another syllable. In words that had become monosyllabic in old (i.e., pre-dialectal) Ossetian, initial and medial *ă (hă) become *o* if

---

[1] *Iron ävzag,* East Ossetic.

[2] *Dįguron ävzag,* West Ossetic.

[3] please see: Hunger (1953), Németh (1958).

[4] please see: Bielmeier (1989), Klaproth (1814).

followed by a consonant cluster starting with *n*. The Old Iranian non-final *a* frequently becomes *i* (in Iron) and *u* (in Digor)[1]. The core of the Ossetian vocabulary derives in large measure from Iranian languages sources, although there exist numerous lexical and idiomatic calques, due to a long-standing influence of neighbor languages. The great number of Iranian languages terms referring to traditional culture testifies to social continuity and coherence in the Alan-Ossetian tribes. A number of Christian terms have been borrowed from Georgian, but there exist apparently traces of old pagan terms that have been used to express Christian notions. Muslim terms have been introduced from Perso-Arabic through the medium of Caucasic neighbor languages. Azeri Turkish which previously functioned widely as a *lingua franca* in the Northeast Caucasus, has been a link connecting the Ossetes with the other North Caucasian peoples, as well as with the Muslims of the south. Moreover, a great number of cultural words have entered Ossetian through Azeri as a direct or indirect source. In modern times, numerous Russian words, mainly technical and political terms, have been borrowed. The kinship terms are mostly with Iranian languages roots.

Tabari Language[2]:
Tabari is an Iranian language of the Northwestern branch. As a member of the Northwestern branch (the northern branch of Western Iranian), etymologically speaking it is rather closely related to Gilaki, and more distantly related to Persian, which belongs to the

---

[1] for details please see: Thordarson (1989).
[2] or Mazani/Mazandarani

Southwestern branch[1]. Tabari and Gilaki enjoy similar vocabularies, and share certain typological features with Caucasian languages[2] reflecting the history, ethnic identity, and close relatedness to the Caucasus region and Caucasian peoples on the southern shores of the Caspian Sea. Tabari has, however, a remarked individuality of its own, and differs from the other Iranian languages in important respects. Spoken in a territory sheltered by the high Alborz mountains in the south and the Caspian sea in the north, Tabari preserves many ancient Indo-European words no longer in common use in modern Iranian languages such as Persian. In linguistic typology, Tabari's normal word order is subject–object–verb (SOV), but in some tenses it may be SVO (subject–verb-object), depending on dialects[3]. Tabari like other modern Iranian languages has no distinction between the dative and accusative cases, and the nominative in the sentence takes almost no indicator. There are some remnants from old Tabari that female nouns in nominative were ending with *a* and male nouns in nominative were ending with *e*[4]; this type of grammatical gender still exists in other close languages such as Semnani, Sangesari and Zazaki. Tabari is an inflected language, therefore many Tabari words might be modified to express different grammatical categories such as tense, case, voice, aspect, person, number, gender, mood, etc.

---

[1] Coughlin, 2006: p. 89.
[2] please see: Nasidze & Others, 2006: pp. 668–673.
[3] for details please see: Johanson (2006).
[4] as in *jǝnā* meaning the woman and *mǝrdē* meaning the man.

It is also a genderless language and no distinctions of grammatical gender, means no categories requiring morphological agreement between nouns and associated pronouns, adjectives, articles, or verbs. Adpositions in Tabari are after words, while most of other modern Iranian languages including Persian have preposition systems in general[1]. Tabari is rich in synonyms, especially reffering to the domestic animals, some such nouns also retaining the gender they possessed in Indo-European times[2]. Among the living Iranian languages, Tabari has one of the longest written traditions, from the 10th to the 15th century. This status was achieved during the long reign of the independent and semi-independent rulers of Tabaristan (Mazandaran) in centuries after the Arab invasion[3]. The rich literature of Tabari language includes books such as *Niki'nūmē* by Marzban-ibn-e-Rostam and his fables' book of *Marzban'nūmē* which was translated into Persian by Saad-ad-Din-Varavini in the 12th century, and *Bavand'nūmē* show the importance of Tabari as a significant language of the *New Era*. The use of Tabari, however, has been in decline. Its literary and administrative rank was lost to Persian perhaps long before the ultimate integration of Tabaristan into the national administration in the early seventeenth century[4].

---

[1] the only common postpositions that sometimes becoming preposition are *še* and *tā*.

[2] example: Miš, Gal, Gerz means mouse, but are not of same gender.

[3] Windfuhr, 1989: pp. 246–249.

[4] Borjian, 2005: pp. 65-73.

Persian Language

Persian gets its name from its origin at the capital of the Achaemenid Empire, Persis, modern-day Fars Province, hence the name Persian (Farsi). It has up to three well known major variants and is primarily spoken in Iran as Farsi (the literal Persian word for it and spoken as a first language by Iranians), in Afghanistan as Dari (officially known as Dari since 1958 and spoken as a *lingua franca* by the majority of the Afghans), and in Tajikistan as Tajiki or Tajik (officially known as Tajiki since the Soviet Era and spoken by the Tajiks of Northern Afghanistan and Tajikistan), and in some other regions which historically were Persianate societies; hence Persian identity is evaluated beyond the boundaries of these countries and regions, these variants are almost entirely mutually intelligible. In more recent times, when Iran and Central Asia became divided religiously and politically, different varieties of Persian emerged, which eventually led to the Tajiki standard; however, the domain of Persian saw a considerable contraction. In Bukhara, a center of Persian for a millennium, the language was replaced by Uzbek as the state language when the Emirate of Bukhara became Soviet Uzbekistan in the early 1920s. It was only in Soviet Tajikistan, carved out of the eastern highlands of Bukhara, that Persian retained its official status under the new name of Tajik[1]. According to the definition of the classical languages, Persian is one; in 1872, at a meeting in Berlin of European linguists and other scholars, Greek, Persian, Latin, and Sanskrit were chosen as the world's classical

---

[1] Borjian, 2015: p. 236.

languages. From a scientific point of view, a language would be considered a classical language, which is primarily ancient, secondarily, rich in literature, and thirdly underwent little change in the last millennium of its existence. Persian is considered one of the richest languages of the Indo-European language family in terms of some linguistic features such as the variety of words and lexical range. Some languages have borrowed Persian lexicons, for instance there are 811 Persian loanwords in English[1]. Persian is now considered as one of the most dynamic and rich languages inheritated by humanity. In the past, much knowledge has been transmitted to the world by this language, and now it has not been diminished; therefore, learning this language means joining to a wide range of human knowledge[2]. One of the major effects of the Persian language on the neighbouring languages is the influx of the Persian proverbs in their contexts, some of them without any changes. In terms of the number and variety of proverbs, Persian is among the three first languages of the world[3]. Today, due to the importance of the Persian language and its penetration rate into other territories, familiarization with this language attracts concerns and is pursued in some research institutes.

New Persian is the predominant modern descendant of Old and Middle Persian and is one of the Western Iranian languages and is known as a pluricentric language. According to available documents, the Persian language is "the only Iranian language" for which close

---

[1] Kaye (2004).
[2] Maze Poua (2003).
[3] Rahmandoost, 2008: Preface.

philological relationships between all of its three stages are established and so that Old, Middle, and New Persian represent one and the same language of Persian. Hence, the Persian language (of the *New Era*) is classified as the direct descendant and the continuation of Middle Persian (of the *Medieval Era*), the official religious and literary language of the Sasanian Empire; itself a continuation of Old Persian (of the *Ancient Era*), the language of the Achaemenid Empire. New Persian has been written in a modified Arabic alphabet at least since the 9th century CE, known as Perso-Arabic alphabetys, and developed an extensive classical literature and became the *lingua franca* of the Iranians and in some neighbouring countries. For eight centuries (1000-1800 CE) Persian played the important role of *lingua franca* in large parts of the Western And Southern Asia with different ethnicities. At the *New Era*, Persian had a major efficacy in the vast empires adjacent to its East and West such as India and the Ottoman Empire and gained influence in their courts. In fact, during this period, Persian has had a considerable influence (mainly lexical) on neighboring languages, particularly the Turkic languages in Central Asia, the Caucasus, and Anatolia, neighboring Iranian languages, as well as Armenian, Georgian, and Indo-Aryan languages. Within this period, Persian expanded up to the Eastern parts of Africa and played an important role in the formation of the Swahili language. In this historic era, Persian sources have been within Greater Iran including present day Iran, Iraq, Afghanistan, the Caucasus and Turkey, Central Asia and South Asia where the Persian language has historically been either the native or official language.

From the literate point of view, during the First Period (of the *Ancient Era*), Persian literature comprises oral compositions and written texts as one of the world's oldest literatures[1]. Described as one of the great literatures of humanity[2], including Goethe's assessment of it as one of the four main bodies of world literature[3], Persian literature has its roots in surviving works of the *Medieval Era*, as well as the *Ancient Era*. Persian literature in the process of passing the *Medieval Era* and reaching the *New Era*, entered the important age of the Early New Persian (ENP)[4]. With a long history of literature in the form of Middle Persian before Islam, Persian was the first language in the Muslim world to break through Arabic's monopoly, and the writing of poetry in Persian was established as a court tradition in many eastern courts. Works of the ENP poetry are characterized by strong court patronage, an extravagance of panegyrics, and what is known as *sabk-e-faxer*[5]. The tradition of royal patronage began perhaps under the Sasanid Age in the *Medieval Era* and carried over through the Abbasid and Samanid courts into every major Iranian dynasty. This tradition continued and bacame a main source to initiate pathways like the Qasida which was perhaps the most famous form of panegyric used, though quatrains such as those in Khayyam's *Ruba'iyyat* became also widely popular in the *New Era*. It seems, through this system of patronage

---

[1] Spooner, 1994: pp. 177–178.; Spooner, 2012: p. 94.; Campbell | King, 2013: p. 1339.

[2] Arberry, 1953: p. 200.

[3] Levinson | Christensen, 2002: p. 480.

[4] ENP will be used to abbreviate the Early New Persian.

[5] exalted in style.

the epic style of poetry emerged, with Ferdowsi's *Šāh-nāma* [1] at the apex. By glorifying the historical past in heroic and elevated verses, Ferdowsi and others such as Daqiqi and Asadi-Tusi presented their works with a source of pride and inspiration that has helped preserve a sense of identity for the People over the ages. By the 14th century, when New Persian standardized and had become widespread, most of the other languages which have been in contact with Persian followed suit[2]. For instance, Rumi, born in Balkh, wrote in Persian and lived in Konya, then the capital of the Saljuqs in Anatolia.

---

[1] composed in the late 10th and early 11th centuries.

[2] as in Judeo-Persian literature, Šāhin from Shiraz, a 14th century poet composed 14,000 couplets in his three major works of *Musā-nāme*, *Berešit-nāme*, *Ardašir-nāme*, and *Ezrā-nāme* (*Ardašir-nāme* and *Ezrā-nāme* can be treated as one book divided into two interrelated sections) followed by Emrāni (1454–1530) -who is surmised to have been from Isfahan and lived in Kashan- with works of *Ganj-nāme*, *Fath-nāme*, and *Ḥanukā-nāme*. Emrāni also composed a *Sāqi-nāme*, a persian genre in which the poet, seeking relief from his discontents, orders the cupbearer (sāqi) to bring him wine. Several poets from central Iran emulated them, the most celebrated is Aminā (the penname of Benyāmin ben Mišāʾil born in Kashan in 1672), known by *Tafsīr of Azhārōt-nāme*, a piece of 324 couplets composed in 1732, and *Monājāt*, and *Davāzdah ševaṭim*. in the 17th century, Aharon ibn Māšiaḥ (an Isfahani settled in Yazd) emulated Emrāni's *Fath-nāme* by using the same style and meter; he also embarked on *Šofṭim-nāme* in the same century, in bukhara, Xwāja-ye Boxārāʾi has *Dāniāl-nāme* (2,175 couplets written in 1606); in Samarkand, Elišaʿ ibn Šamuʾil (pen-name Rāḡeb) wrote *Šāhzāde o Ṣufi* and *Ḥanukā-nāme*, composed on the framework of Emrāni's epic of the same name. In the 19th century, another admired poet was Simān-ṭov Melammed (born in Yazd and moved to Khorasan - pen-name Ṭubiā), best known for his *Azhārōt*, and *Piyyuṭ*.

There is thus Persian literature in Iran, Mesopotamia, the Caucasus, Minor Asia of Anatolia, subcontinent of India, and other parts of Central Asia.

When New Persian literature became widespread in the 14th century, the other languages which have been in contact with Persian followed the Persian prose style[1]. In Persian, after familiarization with Arabic prosody, in the field of literature, most genre of poetry are produced. In prose, the most significant of them are *Chahār-maqāleh* by Arudhi[2], anecdote compendium *Jawami-ul-hikayat* and *Lubab-ul-albab* both by Aufi[3], *Qabus-nama* by Ghaboos[4], and *Siyasat-nama* by Nizam al-Mulk. Translation of *Kelileh-va-demneh*, can also be mentioned in this category. Among the major historical and biographical works *Tarikh-i-beyhaqi* by Beyhaghi, *Tarikh-i-jahangushay-i-juvaini* by Ata-Malik-Juvayni, and *Tazkerat-ol-owliya*[5] by Attar can be named. Even the oldest surviving work of Persian literary criticism -an attempt to evaluate literary works critically[6]- *Muqaddame-ye-*

---

[1] as in Judeo-Persian literature, Bābāi ibn Loṭf wrote *Ketāb-e-anusi* about forced conversion under the policies of the Safavid dynastic rule. A few decades later, Bābāi ibn Farhād pursued the work of his grandfather in *Ketāb-e-sargozašt-e-Kāšān*.

[2] complete name: Nizami Arudhi Samarqandi.

[3] complete name: Zahiriddin Nasr Muhammad Aufi.

[4] complete name: Shams al-Mo'ali Abol-hasan Ghaboos ibn Wushmgir.

[5] biographies of the Saints, a detailed account of Sufi mystics, which is referenced by many subsequent authors and considered a significant work in mystical hagiography.

[6] no single literary criticism has survived from Pre-Islamic Iran, but some Pahlavi essays (*Ayin-e-name-nebeshtan* and *Bab-e-ebtedai-e*) considered as literary criticism (Zarrinkoub, 1959: pp: 374–379).

shah-name-ye-abu-mansuri, is written during the Samanid period of the *New Era*[1]. Although some works like *Karvand* demonstrates before Arab conquere, Iranians had works on eloquence; there are signs that some Persian elite were familiar with Greek rhetoric and literary criticism. The bulk of Persian literature, however, comes from the times following the Abbasids power, when Iranians became the scribers and bureaucrats of this Arab Empire and, increasingly, also its writers and poets. The language of the literature of the New Persian arose and flourished in Khorasan and Chorasmia; as because of political reasons, early Iranian dynasties such as the Tahirids and Samanids being based in Khorasan. Another genre of the literature of the *Medieval Era* which is transferred to the *New Era* and accordingly to the New Persian is storytelling. Although no story is inherited, but relics like tale collection of *hezar-o-yek-shab*[2] about a Queen who must relate a series of stories to her malevolent husband, King Šahryār, shows this genre as a Medieval folk was popular in the *Second Period*. The nucleus of the collection is formed by a Pahlavi book *Hazār Afsānah*[3], a collection of ancient Indian and Persian folk tales. During the *New Era*, in the 8th century —during the earliest stage of ENP - at the time of the Abbasid Caliph when Baghdad had become an important cosmopolitan, and

---

[1] Parsinejad (2003).

[2] the stories which were told over a period of 1001 nights to delay Queen's execution, and every night she ends the story with a suspenseful situation, forcing the King to keep her alive for another day. The individual stories were created over several centuries, by many people from a number of different lands.

[3] Thousand Myths.

merchants and traders from Iran, China, India, Africa, and Europe were practicing there, many of originally folk stories have been collected orally over many years and later compiled into a single book[1]. The frame story of Shahrzad seems to have been added in the 14th century. Not all literature written in Persian is written only by ethnic Persian speakers; as Turkic, Caucasian, and Indic poets and writers have also used the Persian language in the environment of Persianate cultures. In this way, Persian exerted some influence on Arabic as the writing system of Persian language, particularly Bahrani Arabic, while borrowing much vocabulary from it after the Muslim conquest of Iran. In general for centuries, Persian has been a prestigious cultural language in other regions of Western, Central, and South Asia through the various empires based in the regions. At the time of the Gurkanian Empire in India, Persian was the official language of India and speaking Persian was an art and honour for the Indian scholars and literates. In the last century, the collapse of the Ottoman Empire, which considered the Persian language as its administrative language, and Russianization of Central Asia by the Soviet Union authorities which provided the basis for the development of Russian language to the detriment of the Persian language, and to give more value to the English language in the Indian subcontinent, although Persian language encountered serious challenges, but did not reduce its importance[2].

---

[1] The storyteller Abu Abd-Allah Muhammad el-Gahshigar of the 9th century is the Arabic translator.
[2] Pahlavan, 1996: pp. 9-25.

Early New Persian[1]**:** The demise of the Sasanian Empire through Arab invasion (632-51 CE) and the ensuing Islamization of Iran marks a major break in Iranian history, providing Iran with the basis for a new culture and identity. Out of the remnants of the former "national" Iranian culture, the first Persian documents written in Arabic script emerged during the 9th-10th centuries, continuing the Sasanian Middle Persian language in a new garb. Its development of over 200 years was a slow and steady development, betraying many moments of continuity[2]. The distinction between Middle Persian (of the *Medieval Era*) and New Persian (of the *New Era*) is due as much to convention, to extra-linguistic factors such as the historical break, and to changes connected to this break such as the shift of script (from Pahlavi to Perso-Arabic), as to linguistic differences. Hence, for a better understanding of the difference between the Middle Persian and the New Persian (in its latest stage as Modern Persian), there would be a brief explanation of the New Persian in its early stage which is categorised as ENP; its historical background, evolution, important shifts and its grammar. The appearance of this new stage of the Persian language can be apperceived in a time phase of the early 8th century upto the fading out of this stage in the late 12th (or early 13th) century when realistic poetry of the Khorasani style format was changing over to the next style of the mystical Araqi style of Sufi poetry[3].

---

[1] main source: Paul (2018), and Borjian (2015).
[2] Paul (2018).
[3] there is no clear linguistic break between ENP and later stages of

While initially overshadowed by Arabic language during the Umayyad Caliphate and early Abbasid Caliphate, a new phase of the New Persian soon became a literary language of the Central and West Asia. The rebirth of the Persian language in its new form is often accredited to Ferdowsi, then the lyricism of Asjadi, Farrukhi Sistanui, Onsori, Manuchehri, Daqiqi, and Rudaki; the panegyric maestri who were known for their love of nature, their verse abounding with evocative descriptions. Most of these maestros used Pre-Islamic genre as a conduit to revive the language and customs of the ancient age. In the new style of Khorasani, the followers mostly were associated with Greater Khorasan, which is characterized by its supercilious diction, dignified tone, and relatively literate language. Even after centuries, ENP remains largely intelligible to speakers of Modern Persian, as the morphology and, to a lesser extent, the lexicon of the language have remained relatively stable. The linguistic difference between the 7th century Middle Persian and the 10th century ENP is certainly smaller, in many ways, than the one between the 10th century ENP and the 21st century Modern Persian. The definition of this stage followed here corresponds to the one implicitly given by Lazard[1], saying that from the 13th century onwards, dialectal features were declining in Persian documents and a dialectally homogeneous standard of the language was more or less reached. Following this definition, ENP would span the stages of New Persian from its beginning, the 8th century, to approximately the early 13th century.

Persian.

[1] 1963: pp. 18, 24.

A further distinction may be made between a formative phase of this stage which lasted until the early/mid-11th century, when Persian had more or less attained the status of a language of literature, administration, and science, and the ENP of thriving classical literature between the mid-11th and the early 13th century. Even after the 13th century, Persian did not become fixed or standardized, the development of Persian since the 8th century has been continuous and gradual, and instead of speaking of one "classical" standard of the language, one should rather speak of a series of temporary standards of stylistic nature that were set by classical authors such as Ferdowsi, Saedi, or Hafez[1]. Iranian national philology has defined certain stylistic standards in terms of region, time, or dynasty, e.g., the Samanid style of simple the 10th-11th century prose[2], or the Khorasani style of the early 10th-12th centuries realistic poetry. The ending of the Early stage of the New Persian in the early-13th century marks the ascendancy of lyric poetry with the consequent development of the *ghazal* into a major verse form, as well as the rise of mystical Araqi style of Sufi poetry, which is known by its emotional lyric qualities, rich meters, and the relative simplicity of the language. Emotional romantic poetry was not something new however, as works such as *Vis-o-Ramin* by Asad Gorgani, and *Yusof-o-Zoleikha* by Amaq-Bokharai exemplify. The elites of this school are Rumi, Saedi, Hafez, and Sanai, Attar, Khaqani-Shirvani, Anvari, and Nizami also were respected *ghazal* writers. In the didactic genre *Hadiqat-ul-haqiqah* by Sanai and *Makhzan-ul-srār* by Nizami can

---

[1] please also see: Paul (2002).
[2] Rypka, 1968: p. 112.

be mentioned. Some of Attar's and Rumi's works also belong to this genre, although some tend to classify these in the lyrical type due to their mystical and emotional qualities. In addition, some tend to group Naser Khosrow's works in this style as well; however true gems of this genre are two books by Saedi, the *Bustan* and the *Gulistan*. After the 15th century, the Indian style of Persian poetry (Isfahani or Safavi styles) took over. This style has its roots in the Timurid Age and produced the likes of Amir Khosrow Dehlavi. Each of these styles could be emulated by later authors (e.g., the 19th century Qajar poet Qāʾāni wrote in Khorasani style), but they are no "absolute" standards of New Persian. Even *Modern* "Standard Persian" is only a transitory, flexible idiom that continues developing.

Early New Persian Grammar: The stage of ENP was the first phase (8th-12th centuries CE) of the Persian language after the Islamic conquest of Iran. Its grammar is in many ways much simpler than its ancestral forms, having lost most of the inflectional systems of the older varieties. Other than markers to indicate that nouns and pronouns are direct objects, New Persian has no system of case inflections. Possession is shown by addition of a special suffix (the *ezāfeh*) to the possessed noun. Verbs retain a set of personal endings related to those of other Indo-European languages, but a series of prefixes, infixes (word elements inserted within a word), and auxiliary verbs, are used instead of a single complex inflectional system in order to mark tense, mood, voice, and the negative.

Dialectology: For a proper understanding of the evolution of this stage, a closer look at its dialectal situation in the 7th century seems necessary. Most valuable information about this is provided by Ruzbeh (721-57)[1], as transmitted in the 10th century Ibn-al-Nadim's *Fehrest*. According to Ruzbeh, five languages were spoken in late Sasanian Iran, three of which are Iranian: Pahlavi used in central and Northwest Iran, the ancient region of Media[2], Dari spoken at the court of Ctesiphon-Seleucia [3]and in Khorasan, and Pārsi spoken in the province of Fārs and used by the Zoroastrian priests. Lazard (1971) shows Pārsi and Dari are two functional and regional varieties of Persian, Pārsi

---

[1] the Iranian-born polymath Ruzbeh commonly known as Ibn-al-Muqaffa.

[2] Rey, Isfahan, Hamadān, Azerbaijan, Māh Nehāvand.

[3] Arabic: al-Madāen.

representing the literary language, especially that of religious (Zoroastrian) literature, and the regional variety spoken in Southern Iran, and Dari representing the language spoken at court and in the northeast of Iran (including large regions of present-day Afghanistan and Central Asia).

Northwest: In *Pahlavi*, ancient epic traditions were preserved in various regions of Iran, even after Parthian had ceased to be used as an official language. According to Ruzbeh[1], *Pahlavi* -is called Fahla or Bahla in Arabic sources- was spoken in central and Northwest Iran, the ancient region of Media, however, it was not indigenous to that region. The homeland of the Parthians in Arsacid times had been Khorasan[2]; at the end of the Sassanids, Parthian must have been extinct or nearly extinct there.

After the 6th century, Parthian continued to be used only as a language of the Manichean liturgy in Central Asia (along the Silk Road[3]). The public speaking used in central and Northwest Iran and called "Pahlavi" in the 7th century is not likely to be Parthian proper, but more probably a bundle of Parthoid dialects, forerunners of the Northwest Iranian languages and dialects spoken there until today, such as Ṭāleši, Southern Tāti, or variants of Āzari. The semantic development of the term Pahlavī in ENP seems to corroborate this. In Sasanian Age, when Parthian gradually disappeared as a living language, ancient Parthian epics were integrated and assimilated

---

[1] Ibn-al-Nadim, ed. Tajaddod, p. 15; tr. Dodge, I, 1970: p. 24.

[2] Parthian territory for times included Tabaristan and southern parts of today Turkmenistan too.

[3] please see: Sundermann, 1986: p. 315.

to Middle Persian literature[1]. The term *Pahlavī* was now identified with "heroic, old, ancient"[2], and later the name of the bygone Parthian language was transferred to the Persian language written by Zoroastrians that seemed likewise to be ancient or heroic to the Iranian Muslims[3]. Another meaning of *Pahlavī* in ENP, attested later in the Arabicized plural form *fahlaviyāt* and designating poetry in the dialects from the Fahla/Bahla region from the 10th century onwards, is a direct continuation of that of the 7th century "Parthoid" dialects.

Northeast: Khorasan, the homeland of the Parthians (called *abaršahr*), had been partly Persianized already in late Sasanian Age. Following Ruzbeh, the variant of Persian spoken there was called Darī and was based upon the one used in the Sasanian capital Ctesiphon-Seleucia[4]. The regions adjacent to Khorasan, namely, Sogdiana[5], Bactria, and Chorasmia, were Persianized later, after the Arab conquest of Iran—a process that coincided with their Islamization; centuries later, the Persianization of Sogdiana and Chorasmia should be followed by their Turkicization. Under this specific

---

[1] e.g., the Middle Persian *Yadegar-e-zariran* whose Parthian loanwords show that the text was based on a Parthian original.

[2] Lazard, 1972: p. 35.

[3] note that Pahlavī meaning "Zoroastrian-Middle-Persian" developed as an exonym used by Iranian Muslims, while the endonym of the Zoroastrian Persians for their own language continued to be Pārsī(g) for some centuries. It is also believed Pārsī(g) as Sasani Pahlavi (South-West), while Pahlavani(g) as Arsacid Pahlavi (North-West).

[4] Arabic: al-Madāen.

[5] capital: Bukhara.

historical conditions the Middle Persian of the 7th century was developed, within two centuries, to the New Persian that is attested in the earliest specimens of New Persian poetry in the late 9th century. Compared to the Middle Persian, the New Persian has undergone substantial grammatical changes, e.g., it has given up the Middle Persian *eżāfa ī(g)* as a relative clause marker, the indirect (and sometimes direct) object marker *ō*, and the ergative transitive constructions of the past. Compared to the New Persian, which was the result of a historical break, the Pārsi New Persian of Southern Iran remained closer to Zoroastrian-Middle-Persian.

South: The variety of Persian called *Pārsī* by Ruzbeh, spoken in Southern Iran and used as a literary language by the Zoroastrians of Fārs, continued well into Islamic times. Zoroastrian literature in Pārsi[1], thrived during the 8th-9th centuries, perhaps also as a reaction to increasing social and cultural pressure from the Islamic caliphate and its local agents such as the Taherids or Saffarids. The language of the Southern Early-New-Judeo-Persian documents can be considered more or less a continuation of Zoroastrian-Middle-Persian. Up to the 11th or early 12th century, these documents preserved Middle Persian grammatical features and lexemes that had already vanished from contemporaneous New Persian in the northeast, e.g., the eżāfa *i* introducing relative clauses, the preposition *o* "to" (Middle Persian *ō*), or traces of ergativity[2]. There is no evidence to prove that

---

[1] later called "Pahlavi" by Iranian Muslims.
2 Paul, 2013: p. 156.
  in terms of prepositions, the transitory nature of the language reflects there.

the Jews and Zoroastrians of Southern Iran considered the form of Persian they used during the 8th-11th centuries as a *new* form of Persian detached from *late* Middle Persian. They continued to call their language *Pārsī* [1] well into the 11th century and beyond. The "change of paradigm" for the southern varieties of Persian came with the Saljuq dynasty, under whose rule the Islamicized Persian from the northeast was spread to all other parts of Iran as a language of administration, culture, and communication and increasingly influenced all other varieties.

The dialectal basis of the New Persian: New Persian is based on the Persian of Khorasan, and (following Ruzbeh) Dari shares a common dialectal basis with the variety of Middle Persian that was spoken at the former Sasanian court in the capital Ctesiphon-Seleucia; this is likely to have been the basis for literary Manichean-Middle-Persian. All three historical stages of Persian should therefore be dialectally homogeneous; this is, however, not the case. Early-New-Manichean-Persian had more purely preserved its Persian (Southwest Iranian) linguistic type as compared to Zoroastrian-Middle-Persian, the official language of the Sasanian Empire, which had absorbed more lexical influences from Arsacid Parthian, the language of their dynastic predecessors.

New Persian, shares some Zoroastrian-Middle-Persian features of these words "zemestān, pezešk, bāḡ", showing that New Persian is not based solely on Early-New-Manichean-Persian. To explain this, one has to keep in mind that the Persian of the 7th century was not a homogeneous language or dialect, but basically

---

[1] Middle Persian *Pārsīg*.

the spoken variety of Sasanian Persian, as against Pārsi, the language of administration and predominantly Zoroastrian literature; this kind of Persian must have absorbed many influences from Zoroastrian-Middle-Persian and from Parthian during the Sasanian Age, and there must have existed various local varieties or styles of this specific Persian by the 7th century. There are no extant Khorasani Persian documents from the 7th-8th centuries, but it is possible to get an impression of its dialectal non-homogeneity from the later Khorasani or northeastern prose texts of the 10th century including southwestern forms like damestān "winter" from the *Hodud-al-ālam*[1]; or the lexical doublet (h)ēzom/hēma "firewood"[2].

---

[1] Lazard, 1963: p. 54, fn. 8.

[2] Lazard, 1963: p. 166; cf. Zoroastrian-Middle-Persian/Early-New-Manichean-Persian *ēzm/ēmag* 'id.', with *ēzm* being from Parthian; in later New Persian, *hizom* < *(h)ēzom*< *ēzm* prevailed.

Evolution Of Early New Persian

Starting from Ruzbeh's account of the linguistic situation in the 7th century, accounts and statements of other Arabic and Iranian authors about the linguistic situation in 8th-11th centuries Iran serve to complement the information given by Ruzbeh and to follow up on the evolution of Persian during that time. These complementary accounts help to draw a more lively and complete picture of the usage of Persian and of the views of the people on the language(s) they used. It must be borne in mind that language names are not always stable, but may be flexible and subject to semantic change in the course of time. Ruzbeh himself gave a good example of this flexibility. He used the term "Pārsi" in its specific meaning of "Southern Persian" but also as a cover term meaning "Iranian", covering all languages (even non-Iranian ones) that were spoken in Iran[1]; from this meaning, the term Pārsi-(ye-)Dari "the Pārsi (variant, namely) Dari" would later be derived.

Geographical spread: Ruzbeh's opaque remark that Dari was spoken not only in Khorasan, but that the "dominant" variety of Dari was that of Balk, becomes clearer through statements by other authors such as Ṭabāri that Pārsi was spoken in Balk[2], or Naẓr-ibn-Šamil that Pārsi-Dari is the language used in Balk[3]. Balk, thus, must have been an established center of Persian language and culture in early Islamic times. Later, Jāḥeẓ writes that the people of Marv spoke in the sweetest and

---

[1] Lazard, 1971: p. 363.

[2] referring to the situation of 726; Perry, 1991: p. 51.

[3] before 822; Ṣādeqi, 1978: p. 44.

most skillful manner among Iranians[1]; Naršaki, that the Qorān was read in Pārsi in Bukhara[2]; and Ibn-Ḥawqal, that the inhabitants of Bukhara spoke Dari besides Sogdian[3], these statements more probably refer to (Dari) Persian, and attest to the wide spread of Persian in the whole of Eastern Iran in early Islamic times, which had already developed during the Sasanian Age.

Functional load: administration: In the former Sasanian parts of the Umayyad Empire, Arabic replaced Persian only gradually as a language of administration, from the late 7th to the mid-8th century. This is reflected in statements that the administration of Iraq had always been in Pārsi and was, by now, about to be replaced by Arabic[4]. From later times[5], Eṣṭakri reports that the administration is in Arabic, while the Zoroastrian priests still write in Pahlavi [6]and speak in Pārsi[7].

Functional load: literature: The literary reawakening of Persian in Eastern and Northeast Iran, at the courts of the Saffarids and Samanids during the latter half of the 9th and 10th centuries, is also well reflected in quotations. The Saffarid ruler Yaequb Lays, who did not understand Arabic, ordered one of his viziers to translate an Arabic poem into Persian[8]. Similar motifs are attested from

---

[1] before 868; Lazard, 1971: p. 381.

[2] 953; Lazard, 1971: p. 372.

[3] 973; Ṣādeqi, 1978: p. 49.

[4] Balāḏori, Jahšiāri; Lazard, 1971: p. 369; both authors wrote in the late 9th and early 10th centuries, but their statements refer to the 8th century.

[5] early 10th century.

[6] now Middle Persian.

[7] Lazard, 1971: pp. 365, 379.

[8] 870; *Tārik-e-Sistān*, pp. 209-210.

various authors at the Samanid court, where Persian literature was actively promoted. In his preface to the *Šāh-nāma*, Abu-Manṣur explains that the ruler ordered old epics that had been translated from Middle Persian into Arabic to be translated into New Persian, so that the text would "reach the people"[1]. For the same reasons, Balami translated parts of the *Tārik-e-Ṭabari* into Persian[2], and Meysari decided to write a medical poem in Persian rather than Arabic, because it would be thus understood by a larger audience[3]. The majority of ENP sources which are literary and extant in the form of manuscripts in Arabic scripts, may conveniently be grouped according to their religious affiliation(s):

Poetry: Islamic Persian literature starts with poetry[4]. The earliest works of Persian poetry known today go back to the mid-9th century[5]. No old and independent manuscripts of these poets' works are extant, probably in part because at that time the oral transmission of poetry still predominated; they are known only from short quotations in later collective works such as the lexicography of *Loḡat-e-foros*[6] or the anthology of *Lobāb-al-albāb* (a reliable chronological source)[7]. Despite its old age, ENP poetry is less important linguistically for the study of the evolution of New Persian than other forms

---

[1] 957; Qazvini, 1953: p. 33.

[2] 963; Lazard, 1971: p. 374.

[3] 978; Lazard, 1971: p. 371.

[4] Lazard, 1975: p. 595.

[5] e.g., Ḥanẓala Bādḡisi or Moḥammad-ibn-Waṣif; Lazard, 1964: Pt. I, pp. 17-18.

[6] Asadi Ṭusi (mid-11th century).

[7] Zahiriddin Nasr Muhammad Aufi (early-13th century).

of ENP, especially prose literature. In poetry, national epics are more important linguistically for the study of the evolution of New Persian than other forms of poetries, although epopee does not have the importance of prose literature in studying ENP.

Epics: The Iranian national epic *Šāh-nāma* is of paramount importance for the study of ENP. Its historic and mythic contents had been collected from older compilations such as the Middle Persian *Xwadāy-nāmag*. Ferdowsi based his monumental work on a prose version (now lost) collected under the Dehqān and temporary Samanid governor of Ṭus, Abu Manṣur[1], integrating also parts from an epic of the earlier poet Daqiqi[2]. The language of the *Šāh-nāma* is different from that of contemporaneous poetry or prose: incorporating also "Parthian" epic material, it contains a lot of Parthian loanwords, not all of which found their way later into "standard" Persian[3]. It shares certain grammatical features with ENP texts of Northeast Iranian provenance[4], but retains its own characteristics. Being a compilation of older material, the percentage of Arabic loanwords in the *Šāh-nāma* is lower than in contemporaneous poetical or prose works. The *Šāh-nāma* stands out as the Iranian national epic that reconciles Iranian myths, legends, and traditions with the predominant Islamic culture of the time.

Prose: For ENP prose texts, Lazard's seminal study of 1963 remains the reference work that lists all extant ENP

---

[1] complete name: Abu-Manṣur-ibn-Abd-al-Razzāq.
[2] de Blois, 1997: pp. 105-108.
[3] e.g., *borz* 'high', *pur* 'son', later New Persian *bālā, pəsar*.
[4] e.g., the perfect tense of the type *kardastam*.

prose works of linguistic interest, namely 47 texts of the earlier period (until 1090) and 24 texts from the late 11th and 12th centuries. They include the well-known "classical" texts that made Persian develop into a language of scholarship and prose literature during the 10th-11th centuries, in such fields as historiography, medicine/pharmacy, astrology, philosophy, and "wisdom literature". Lazard provides ample information about each text, the manuscripts in which it has been transmitted, and its linguistic value. A selection of works serves to illustrate how Persian was gradually coming of age as an Islamic literary language in the course of the 10th and 11th centuries. The Arabic original of the *Tārik-e-Ṭabari* was compiled until 915 by Abu-Jaʿfar-Moḥammad-Jarir-e-Ṭabari, at a time when no one yet conceived of Persian as a language of Islamic learning or scholarship. Fifty years later, a need was felt to translate into Persian those parts of the *Tārik-e-Ṭabari* that pertained to the Iranian past, a task entrusted by the Samanid Manṣur ibn Nuḥ to his vizier Balʿami. It seems that historiography, important for the rulers to refer to a heroic past of their dynasty, paved the way for other scholarly disciplines, such as medicine or astrology, to be written down. Persian prose literature of the second half of the 10th century mainly consisted of translations from Arabic works or of works written on the basis of Arabic sources. This changed slowly during the first half of the 11th century. The Chorasmian polymath Biruni still expressed a strong preference for Arabic over Persian as a language of scholarship. Around 1030, he nevertheless composed one of his works, the astrological *Tafhim*, in Arabic and Persian. The celebrated Iranian-Islamic scholar and philosopher Avicenna also wrote most of his works in Arabic, but around 1030 he likewise chose to write at least one of his major philosophical works, the *Dāneš-nāma*, in Persian, and even made an effort to create Persian equivalents to philosophical terms that had hitherto existed only in Arabic. In the second half of the 11th century, when the Saljuq dynasty had taken power in the caliphate, Persian had already been established as a language of literature and science, and increasingly of administration. The high prestige of Persian as an Islamic language on equal right with Arabic is illustrated by the *Siāsat-nāma* written by the Saljuq vizier Neẓām-al-Molk in 1091, which is the most important example of "wisdom literature", or a "mirror of princes", in Islamic literatures. Comprising ancient Iranian (Sasanian) governmental traditions, this genre goes back to Arabic works written by the Iranian genius Ruzbeh in the 8th century.

Epigraphy: ENP inscriptions are very scarce and short and provide little evidence for the linguistic development of Persian. The earliest extant inscription is that on a silver bowl from the 9th century; the earliest monumental inscriptions are from the mid-11th century, on buildings in the Qarakhanid territory[1]. The Samanids, who actively promoted the development of Persian literature, do not yet seem to have questioned the priority of Arabic over Persian in their monuments and artifacts[2].

---

[1] i.e., in the periphery of the Islamic-Iranian world.
[2] O'Kane, 2009: pp. 11-12, 17, 25.

Investigating the grammar of the ENP stage, one must bear in mind that there cannot be one grammar of ENP, because this stage of Persian was not a unified language during the 8th-12th centuries. Due to the disintegration of Iran and of Persian culture and language after the Islamic conquest of Iran, there was a great variety of Persian dialects during this period. They are usually grouped as those of the northeast, where Persian evolved as an Islamic literary language called Dari, and the south, where it continued the variety of Middle Persian called Pārsi.

Vowels: The ENP system of vowels, which also differs remarkably little from the Middle Persian is: *ā ē ī ō ū; a (e) i (o) u.* The Modern Persian Grammar has six vowels, all are produced by egressive pulmonic air-stream. Persian vowels are either simple or compound. Based on the definition, the quality of a simple vowel is the same throughout its articulation period, while the quality of a compound vowel changes during its articulation, so that the change of quality can easily be felt[1].

/æ/	أ ، ‗ ، ‗
/ɒː/	ا ، آ
/ə/	إ ، ‗ ، ه
/iː/	ای ، ‗ی
/o/	أ ، ‗ ، و
/uː/	او ، ـُو

---

[1] Samareh, 1985: p. 101.

Haghshenas[1] classifies Persian vowels based on the primary articulation in three stages: 1) Lips' Shapes, 2) Tongue's Height, and 3) Tongue's Role in Articulation.

1) Vowels in terms of the Lips' Shapes: Meshkatoddini[2] has divided Persian vowels in terms of Lips' Shapes into two groups:

A) Rounded Vowels including: /ɑ, o, u/,

B) Unrounded Vowels including: /a, e, i/.

2) Vowels in terms of Tongue's Height: Meshkatoddini[3] has divided Persian vowels into three categories according to the Tongue's Height:

A) Closed Vowels including: /i, u/,

B) Half-Close Vowels including: /e, o/,

C) Open Vowels including: /ɑ, a/.

3) Vowels in terms of Tongue's Role in Articulation (that part of the tongue that plays an active role in articulation): Meshkatoddini[4] has divided Persian vowels in view of the place of articulation into two categories of Front and Back vowels:

A): Front vowels including: /a, e, i/,

B) Back vowels including: /ɑ, o, u/.

Three vowels /æ/and/ə/and/o/ are traditionally referred to as 'short' vowels and the other three /ɒː/and/iː/and/uː/ as 'long' vowels. In fact the three 'short' vowels are short only when in an open syllable (i.e. a syllable ending in a vowel) that is non-final (but can be stressed or unstressed):

e.g. صدا [sədɒː] 'sound', خدا [xodɒː] 'God'.

---

[1] 2009: p. 99.

[2] 1985: p. 23.

[3] 1985: p. 22.

[4] 1985: p. 21.

When the short vowels are in open syllables, they are unstable and tend in informal styles to assimilate in quality to the long vowel:

شلوغ [ʃolu:ʤ] 'crowded' becomes [ʃu:lu:ʤ],

رسیدن [ræsi:dæn] 'to arrive' becomes [rəsi:dæn][1].

Figure (1) and Table (1) show Modern Persian vowels:

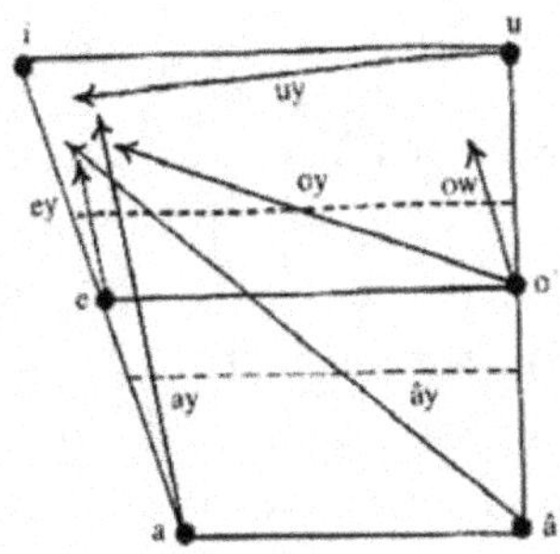

Figure (1): The oral vowel phonemes of Modern Persian according to Samareh (1985: p. 123)

	Front		Central (Medium)		Back	
	UR	Rounded	UR	Rounded	UR	Rounded
Close	i					u
Half-Close	e					o
Half-Open						
Open	a					ɑ

Table (1) Modern Persian Vowels (UR=Unrounded)

---

[1] Toosravandani, 2004: pp. 241–251.

Samareh[1] also believes description and classification of vowels can be based on three principles: 1) distance between the tongue to the mouth ceiling or the degree of the tongue height; 2) that part of the tongue involved in the vowel articulation; 3) lips shape when articulating vowels. The word-final /o/ is rare except for تو /to/ ('you' [singular]), loanwords (mostly of Arabic origin), and proper and common nouns of foreign origin. Word-final /æ/ is very rare in Modern Persian, an exception being نه /næ/ ('no'). The word-final /æ/ in ENP mostly shifted to /ə/ in Modern Persian - often romanized as ⟨eh⟩, meaning [e] is also an allophone of /æ/ in word-final position in Modern Persian - but is preserved in the Eastern dialects. ENP inherited from Middle Persian eight vowels; three short: *i, a, u* and five long: *ī, ē, ā, ō, ū* (in IPA: /i a u/ and /iː eː aː oː uː/). It is likely that this system passed into the common Persian era from a purely quantitative system into one where the short vowels differed from their long counterparts also in quality: *i* > /ɪ/; *u* > /ʊ/; *ā* > /ɑː/. These quality contrasts have in Modern Persian varieties become the main distinction between the two sets of vowels[2]. The inherited eight-vowel inventory is retained without major upheaval in Dari, the only systematic innovation being the lowering of the lax close front *i* and *u* to mid vowels /ə/ and /o/. In Western Persian, two of the vowel contrasts have been lost: those between the tense mid and close vowels. Thus *ē, ī* have merged as /iː/, while *ō, ū* have merged as /uː/. In addition, similarly to

<hr>

[1] 1985: p. 100.
[2] Rees (2008).

Dari, the lax close vowels have become mid: *i* > /e/, *u* > /o/. The lax open vowel has become fronted: *a* > /æ/, and in word-final position further raised to /e/. In both varieties *ā* is more or less labialized. Tajiki has also lost two of the vowel contrasts, but differently from Western Persian: here the tense/lax contrast among the close vowels has been eliminated. That is, *i*, *ī* have merged as /i/, and *u*, *ū* have merged as /u/. The other tense back vowels have shifted as well. Mid *ō* has become more front: /ɵ/ or /ʉ/, a vowel usually romanized as *ů*. Open *ā* has become a mid, labial vowel /o/. The following chart summarizes the later shifts into Modern Tajiki, Dari, and Western Persian[1]:

Early New Persian	Dari Persian	Western Persian	Tajiki Persian
/a/	/æ/	/æ/	/æ/
/aː/	/ɒː/	/ɒː/	/ɔː/
/i/	/e/	/e/	/i/
/iː/	/iː/	/iː/	/i/
/ə/	/ə/	/iː/	/ə/
/aj/	/æj/	/ej/	/æj/
/u/	/o/	/o/	/u/
/uː/	/uː/	/uː/	/u/
/oː/	/oː/	/uː/	/ɵː/
/aw/	/æw/	/ow/	/æw, æv/

---

[1] Windfuhr, 1979: p. 137.

Diphthongs: In Middle Persian, short *e* and *o* were probably marginal phonemes[1]. In Modern Persian, ENP *i/u* have been shifted to *e/o*, and the *majhūl* vowels *ē/ō* to *i/u*. More importantly, vowel length is no longer the main distinctive factor of the vowel system in Modern Persian, but place of articulation, the New Persian system being *ā* (=[å]) *i u / a e o*. The distinction of *a/ā* may be neutralized in ENP, especially in such phonetic environments as before *h*[2]. The status of diphthongs in Modern Persian is disputed[3]. Some linguists list *ei̯, ou̯, āi̯, oi̯, ui̯*,[4]; others list only two *ei̯* and *ou̯*, while some who do not recognize diphthongs in Modern Persian at all[5&6,7]. A major factor that complicates the matter is the change of two classical and pre-classical Persian diphthongs: *ai̯* > *ei̯*, and *au̯* > *ou̯*. This shift occurred in Iran but not in some modern varieties (particularly of Afghanistan)[8]. Morphological analysis also supports the view that the alleged Persian diphthongs are combinations of the vowels with /j/and/w/[9]. The Modern Persian orthography does not distinguish between the diphthongs and the consonants /j/and/w/; that is, they are both written with ی and و respectively.

---

[1] MacKenzie, 1967: p. 23.

[2] Paul 2013: p. 28.

[3] Windfuhr, 1979: p. 137; and Alamolhoda, 2000: pp. 14–15.

[4] Windfuhr, 1979: p. 137.

[5] Windfuhr, 1979: p. 137.

[6] Alamolhoda, 2000: pp. 14–15.

[7] for more information, please refer to: Modarresi Ghavvami (2011).

[8] Windfuhr, 1979: p. 137.

[9] Alamolhoda, 2000: pp. 14–15.

Consonants:

The phonemic system of ENP is remarkably similar to the systems of Middle Persian and Modern Persian.
ENP consonants are shown in Table (2):

	Labial	Dental	Palatal	Velar	Glottal	Laryngeal
Stop	p	t	č	k	q	ʾ
	b	d	j	g		
Fricative	f	s	š		ḵ ḵʷ h	
	(δ)	z (δ)	ž	γ		
Nasal	m	n				
Glide	w	r l	y			

Table (2): Consonants of the ENP

Modern Persian consonants are as follows:

/p, b, t, d, k, ɟ, G, ʔ, f, v, s, z, ʃ, ʒ, x, h, ʧ, ʤ, m, n, l, ɹ, j/

The rather minor grammatical developments from Middle Persian to New Persian are the incomplete merger of [xw] with [x]; acceptance of [ž] as a phoneme; introduction of the guttural stops [q] and [ʾ], possibly as allophones; and the ephemeral fricatives [β] and [δ] in some early dialects of New Persian.

The most important deviation from the Middle Persian system includes the ENP additional stop *q*, and the glottal stop (ʾ), both taken over from Arabic loanwords, and the voiced fricatives *β* and *δ*, probably allophones of *b* and *d* respectively. The bilabial fricative *β* results from a lenition of *b* after a vowel and before a voiced consonant. Its distinct pronunciation appears most clearly from an *f* written with three dots in certain Eealy-New-Arabic-Persian manuscripts[1]. In intervocalic position, *b* may further become lenited to the bilabial semivowel *w*[2]. The phonemic distinction between *b* and *w* is thus weakened, or partly neutralized, in certain Eealy-New-Arabic-Persian dialects, *β* showing an intermediate stage between *b* and *w* and being an allophone of *b*. The *b* may alternate with bilabial glide *w* also word-initially, in words starting with Middle Persian *w-* e.g., '*bahā/wahā* =price' and '*barzeš/warzeš* =training' in Eealy-New-Arabic-Persian [3] and '*bāyenda/wāyenda* =bird' in Eealy-New-Judeo-Persian. A pronunciation of *w* as [β] in this position is also possible. The influx of Arabic loanwords into Persian, 'importing' a clear distinction between *w* and *b* into the language, may have contributed to the stabilization of this distinction in ENP[4]. Etymological study of this case is shown in the voiced bilabial glide of *w* in the word '*wind*' in English, the voiced labiodental fricative of *v* in the word '*vā*' as its equivalent in Tabari, and the voiced bilabial stop of *b* in the word of '*bād*' in Modern Persian, as their homogeneous pair. Postvocalic *d* was written with letter *δāl* and pronounced [δ] in words of Iranian origin in many Eealy-New-Arabic-Persian manuscripts up to the 13th century. It may be considered an allophone

---

[1] e.g., '*aβzūdan* =increase'; Lazard, 1963: p. 1.
[2] e.g., '*biyāwān* =desert'; Lazard, 1963: p. 5.
[3] Lazard, 1963: p. 8.
[4] Pisowicz, 1985: pp. 119-20.

of *d* in this position, and it was shifted back to [d] from the 13th century onwards, probably under the influence of certain Northeastern Persian dialects that had always preserved [d][1]. In words of Arabic origin, however, *d* and *δ* were always kept distinguished in all positions; cf. '*badr* =full moon' vs. '*baδr* =seed'. This led de Blois[2] to assume that *d* and *δ* were separate phonemes in Eealy-New-Arabic-Persian, with their distinction 'imported' into ENP through Arabic loanwords. If Persians, however, pronounced postvocalic **d* as [δ] in words of Persian origin, they probably pronounced postvocalic *d* in Arabic words likewise, the written *dāl* here being due to the conservatism of the script. A postvocalic pronunciation of *d* [d] may have existed in Arabic loanwords, if at all, only in 'learned' pronunciation. The Semitic letter *dālet* may represent both postvocalic stop *d* and fricative *δ*; the occasional writing of postvocalic *d* as *ḍ* in a few Eealy-New-Judeo-Persian documents, however, further corroborates its pronunciation as [δ][3]. Today, some accents and dialects of Modern Persian use [δ] instead of *d* [d]. [4]The lenition of *b* and *d* may already have started in Middle Persian, but it was certainly not phonemic there. The velar fricative *γ* (< **g*) should, however, be considered a phoneme already in Middle Persian, even if it is attested only in Zoroastrian-Middle-Persian, and mostly in loanwords from Avestan and Parthian. The most

---

[1] with a few exceptions like '*guδaštan* =pass'; Pisowicz, 1985: pp. 107 ff.; Meier, 1981: pp. 103-113.

[2] de Blois: 2006, p. 94.

[3] Paul, 2013: p. 16.

[4] a comprehensive discussion of the issue of *d/δ* is given in Filippone; please see: Filippone: (2011), pp. 184-89.

important phonetic and phonemic changes from ENP stage to later stages of New Persian include the followings: 1- The pronunciation of *wāw* shifted from a bilabial glide [w] to a labiodental fricative [v], possibly due to Turkic influence[1]. 2- *k̲ʷ*, which should be considered a phoneme in Middle Persian and ENP, lost its labial component (e.g., '*k̲ʷār* =mean' → [*k̲ār*], except for *k̲ʷa* which turned into *k̲u*, later *k̲o*; e.g., '*k̲ʷads* =self'/→ [*k̲od*]). 3- The ENP distinct phonemes *ġ* and *q* turn into positional allophones with post-velar articulation in Modern Persian, especially in the prestigious variety spoken in the capital Tehran (word-initially and before consonants [q], between two vowels fricative [ġ]). In 'learned' pronunciation and in many areas such as Yazd, Kerman, and Kabul, the two sounds may still be distinguished. The Zoroastrian-Middle-Persian consonant clusters with *s* or *š* as a first element like Zoroastrian-Middle-Persian '*stadan* =take' show a prothetic *i-* already in the Early-New-Manichean-Persian (*istadan*), and both prothetic and anaptyctic *i* side by side in ENP[2](*istadan, sitadan*). In later forms of Persian, there is a preponderance of anaptyctic forms[3], with very few prothetic exceptions. Another feature of this stage is the partial preservation of initial *a-* of many Middle Persian words that would regularly be dropped in later New Persian, where both varieties of ENP represent an intermediate stage of the dropping process (e.g., Middle Persian '*abar*=upon', ENP *(a)bar*, New Persian *bar*)[4].

---

[1] Pisowicz, 1985: p. 120.

[2] Lazard, 1963: p. 105; Paul, 2013: p. 47.

[3] Modern Persian *setadan*.

[4] Lazard, 1963: p. 108; Paul, 2013: p. 46.

Orthography:
The vast majority of Modern Persian in Iran and Afghanistan texts are written with a modified variant of the Arabic script which uses different pronunciation and additional letters not found in Arabic. After the Muslim conquest of Persia, it took approximately two centuries to adopt the Arabic script in place of the older alphabet.

After series of historical changes in the Modern Persian writing system, short vowels are usually not written and only the long ones are represented in the text, and the reader must determine the word from context. The Arabic system of vocalization marks known as *harakat* is also used in Persian, although some of the symbols have different pronunciations. There are several letters generally only used in Arabic loanwords, these letters are pronounced the same as similar Persian letters; hence in Modern Persian there are four functionally identical letters for /z/, whereas in Arabic[1] they are:

/ð ذ/, /z ز/, /dˤ ض/, /ðˤ ظ/;
and three letters for /s/:
/θ ث/, /s س/, /sˤ ص/;
and two letters for /t/:
/t ت/, /tˤ ط/;
and two letters for /h/:
/ħ ح/, /h ه/.
On the other hand, there are four letters that don't exist in Arabic: (/p پ/, /tʃ چ/, /ʒ ژ/, /g گ/).
Tajiki, which is influenced by Russian and the Turkic languages of Central Asia, is written in the Cyrillic script. The Cyrillic script was introduced under the Tajik Soviet

---

[1] Arabic modern standard dialects.

Republic in the late 1930s, replacing the Latin alphabet that had been used since the October Revolution and the Persian script that had been used earlier. After 1939, materials published in the Persian script were banned from the country. There also exist several romanization systems for Persian. The International Organization for Standardization has published a standard for simplified transliteration of Persian into Latin, ISO 233-3, titled 'Information and documentation – Transliteration of Arabic characters into Latin characters – Part 3: Persian language – Simplified transliteration' but the transliteration scheme is not in widespread use. Fingilish is Persian using ISO basic Latin alphabet, which is most commonly used in cyberspace and applications. The orthography is not standardized, and varies among writers and even media (for example, typing 'aa' for the [ɒ] phoneme is easier on computer keyboards than on cellphone keyboards), resulting in smaller usage of the combination on the latter.

Morphology: While Old Persian (as a language belonging to the *Ancient Era*) was a highly inflecting language of the ancient Indo-European type, Middle Persian (as a language belonging to the *Medieval Era*) had given up most categories of nominal, and was about to give up most categories of verbal, inflexion. In Middle Persian, most case relations were expressed by prepositions, and a totally new, synthetic system of verbal tenses was about to be established. The ENP (as a language belonging to the *New Era*) and later New Persian tense systems can be seen as continuations of that of Middle Persian, even if not all details can as yet be fully explained.

Nouns: In the earliest Middle Persian texts from the 3rd-4th centuries, a case distinction for relationship nouns in the singular still existed, e.g., *brād*, '*brādar* =brother'[1]. In later Zoroastrian-Middle-Persian, both *brād* and *brādar* still occur side by side, but they are used indiscriminately, without case distinction. The plural of ENP nouns is marked by the suffixes *-(g)ān* (<Middle Persian) and *-(i)hā*; the latter goes back to a Middle Persian adverbial ending *–īhā*, the *-i-* was dropped in later stages of Persian. The distribution of *-(g)ān* and *-(i)hā* is the same in all varieties of ENP and Modern Persian; *-(g)ān* is used for animate and a small number of other nouns such as plants and body parts[2], and *-(i)hā* is used for all other nouns. In Modern Persian, *-hā* shows a tendency to be generalized at the expense of *-(g)ān*, especially in colloquial registers. The particle *-ē* (< Middle Persian *-ēw*) gives the sense of indefiniteness and unit when attached to an ENP noun. It is called *yā-ye waḥdat/nakara* in Persian grammar and seems to be used in this stage less often than in later stages of the language. Its specifying function, i.e., indicating restrictive relative clauses (*yā-ye ešārat*), seems to be also largely absent from ENP and to have evolved only in later New Persian[3]. Arabic words were borrowed into Persian in great numbers especially during the ENP epoch. Among the borrowings, nouns ending in *-a(t)* (with *tā' marbūṭa*) constitute a large and important section. The

---

[1] Sundermann, 1989: p. 154, with literature.
[2] e.g., '*deraḵtān* =trees'; Lazard, 1963: p. 149.
[3] please see: Lazard, 1966.

borrowings were mostly literary and words in -*a(t)* were borrowed more often in the construct state (-*at*) than in pausa form (-*a*, later -*e*). Perry (1991) has shown in a comprehensive study how in the history of Persian there is a tendency of Arabic borrowings in -*at* to cross over to the -*a/-e*-group; this is not a purely phonetic development, but a complex process involving also semantic, syntactic, and other factors.

Adjectives: While many ENP adjectives cannot be recognized as such formally[1], there are some suffixes that derive adjectives from nouns, such as −*ōmand (mand)*, -*ēn*, -*ī*[2]. The most widespread suffix denoting general relationship in this stage (and later New Persian) is −*ī* (Middle Persian −*īg*)< also as a *nesba* suffixed to places of origin. Material adjectives like *āhanēn* show an interesting development in the history of New Persian: in Modern Persian they are used only metaphorically[3], while the concrete material meaning has been shifted to the -*ī*- suffix ('*dar-e āhani* =iron door')[4]. ENP adjectives usually follow the noun they qualify with an *eżāfa*, but there are exceptions such as quantifying, indefinite, or interrogative adjectives, or superlatives, that precede the noun[5]. Certain frequent qualifying adjectives such as 'good' and 'bad', 'big' and 'small' may also precede the noun in ENP[6]. This shows as an intermediate stage between Middle Persian, where the position of adjectives

---

[1] e.g., '*bozorg* =big'.

[2] '*ziyānōmand* =harmful', '*āhanēn* =(made)of iron', '*arzānī* =worthy'.

[3] '*erāde-ye āhanin* =iron will'.

[4] please see: Paul (2009).

[5] e.g., '*bas* =many', '*čand* =several; how many'; '*bisyār* =many', however, follows the noun; please see: Paul, 2013: p. 101.

[6] Lazard, 1963: p. 165 ff.

was quite free[1], and Modern Persian, where the pre-noun position of adjectives is restricted to quantifying and interrogative adjectives, and superlatives, among others. The comparative adjectives of this stage are normally built by the suffix -*tar*. In all ENP sources, however, old Middle Persian comparative forms without -*tar* still exist, sometimes side-by-side with forms with secondary -*tar*. In Modern Persian, there are only comparatives with -*tar*. Some Middle Persian quantifying adjectives have been preserved in this stage -that no longer exist in Modern Persian-, e.g., '*abārī* =other'[2]; others like ENP '*bas*=many (futher *basī*)' have preserved their Middle Persian meaning as against Modern Persian '*bas* =enough'.

Pronouns: The ENP enclitic pronouns may be attached to any other part of speech (noun, adjective, preposition, verb, conjunction) and serve any possible syntactic function (including, although seldom, that of subject). As shown in Table (4), Middle Persian and Modern Persian suffixes differ from each other:

	Middle Persian	Modern Persian
Sg. 1	- um	- am
Sg. 2	- ut	- at / - et
Sg. 3	- iš	- aš / - eš
Pl. 1	- imān	- emān
Pl. 2	- idān	- etān
Pl. 3	- išān	- ešān

Table (4) Modern Persian Enclitic Pronouns

---

[1] Boyce, 1964: p. 44.
[2] Middle Persian *abārīg*; Lazard, 1963: p. 266; Paul, 2013: p. 100.

Verbs: While there had been a decisive break in the verbal system from Old Persian (of the *Ancient Era*) to Middle Persian (of the *Medieval Era*), with many tenses and moods (like perfect, aorist, optative) having been given up or reduced to a marginal status, the verbal system of Middle Persian seems to be similar to that of New Persian (of the *New Era*) and futher to the Modern Persian at a first look, with ENP taking an intermediate position. All Middle Persian and New Persian verbal forms are based on two stems, present and past, going back to the OIr. present stem and past participle respectively. With the help of auxiliary verbs and verbal particles, a complex system of tenses and moods develops in New Persian, whose details vary greatly from Middle Persian to the stage of ENP, within this stage, and from this stage to later stages of New Persian. In verbal stem formation, there are many dialect variations in ENP stage; e.g., past stems in *-īd* are more widely used in certain texts of ENP stage than they are in later stages of New Persian (e.g., ENP '*oftīdan* =fall' and '*estīdan* =stand' instead of *oftādan* and *estādan*)[1].

Present tense: The ENP present indicative continues the Middle Persian one, which was built from the plain present stem. The adverb *hamē* (later *mē*) could still complement the present verb of this stage with an almost free position in the clause to give it a durative or progressive sense, and the particle/preverb *be* could precede the ENP present verb to emphasize its syntactic autonomy [2]or, in the case of verbs of motion, to modify

---

[1] Lazard, 1963: p. 333; Paul, 2013: p. 125.e.
[2] Lazard, 1963: p. 403; Paul, 2013: p. 144.

its semantics[1].

Both *(ha)mē* and *be* would be grammaticalized as markers of the present indicative or subjunctive only in the course of the 10th-13th centuries; their usage in this stage is rather stylistic, and often unpredictable. The Middle Persian present subjunctive was preserved in this stage in the third singular only, in the hortative ending -*ād*, e.g., '*āf(a)rīn pa šumā bād* =may blessing be upon you'[2]. In modern stage of New Persian, it continues to exist in fossilized expressions like '*mabād-ā* =may it not be'. In later stages of New Persian, the -*ē* (> *i*) was used mainly in conditional clauses of the type '*agar raftami* =if I had gone', and it is no longer used in Modern Persian. There is a 'hortative' particle Early-New-Manichean-Persian *hēb* going back to the Zoroastrian-Middle-Persian *ē(w)* that occurs with present indicative verbs.

Past tenses: Although the Middle Persian, New Persian and ENP systems of past tenses are based mainly on a combination of the past stem, or the past participle, with various suffixes and auxiliary verbs, there are substantial changes of the verbal system from Middle Persian to Early stage of New Persian and from this stage to Modern Persian; the ENP varieties also differ greatly from one another. The Middle Persian simple past ('*āmad hēm* =I came', etc.) is amalgamated into simple past '*āmadam* =I came'. For transitive verbs, this formal amalgamation went along with a syntactic change of paradigm from the ergative to the accusative system[3].

---

[1] *ravad* 'he goes' ~ *be ravad* 'he goes away'; Lazard, 1963: p. 405.

[2] Paul, 2013: p. 146; Lazard, 1963: p. 474.

[3] Middle Persian *kušt hēm* '(he) killed me' > Early New Persian *kuštam* 'I killed'.

From late Middle Persian ergative constructions, it would seem that the formal amalgamation of the endings preceded the transition from ergative to accusative, although this process need not have happened simultaneously in all regions of Iran[1]. Besides the simple past ('*āmadam* =I came'), there are various compound tenses in ENP, the evolution of some of which has not yet been adequately explained. The ENP Past Participle in -*a* may be combined with auxiliary verbs to form paradigms like *rafta buvam, rafta bāšam, rafta hastam,* etc., yielding more or less the same sense as '*raftaam* =I have gone' (but '*rafta bām* is subjunctive =I may have gone')[2]; these forms occur seldom also with the plain past stem (e.g., *āmad bāšad*)[3]. The verbal particle *be* and the adverb *(ha)mē* could be combined freely with all past tenses in ENP, e.g., '*beraftam, berafta buvam, hamē raftastam*', etc., and also with -*ē(h)*, e.g., '*hamē raftand-ē* =they would have gone'[4]. For their usage and meaning with past verbs, the same is as has been explained for the present tenses; an example of verbs of 'low syntactic autonomy' that would be used rather without *than* with *be,* are '*guftan* =say' and '*dīdan* =see' followed by object clauses[5]. Before the plain verb (e.g., *raftam*) became the simple past tense in later New Persian, the prefixed forms (*beraftam*) were used in the same sense for a long time in ENP and later stages of New Persian. There is a great variety of forms of the substantive verb ('to be') in ENP.

---

[1] Paul (2008).
[2] Lazard, 1963: p. 482-83.
[3] Lazard, 1963: p. 485.
[4] Paul, 2013: p. 162.c.
[5] Paul, 2013: p. 159.

The ENP modal verbs ('*(a)bāyed* =it is necessary,' '*šāyed* =it is possible, one can', '*dānistan* =be able', '*ḵʷāstan* =want' etc.) correspond largely to their Middle Persian predecessors, with the exception of ENP '*tawānistan* =can, be able', which is a new formation from the Middle Persian adjective '*tawān* =(it is) possible'. Invariable *(a)bāyēd* and *šāyēd* are used in impersonal constructions and *dānistan, ḵʷāstan* and *tawānistan* are used personally; as in Middle Persian, all these verbs are usually complemented by the infinitive. The most important ENP participles include the passive one (past participle in -*a*), primarily used in compound past tenses, and the three active participles that are built from the present stem with -*anda*, -*ā* (< Middle Persian -*āg*), and –*ān*, the one with -*anda* is mostly used adjectivally in Middle Persian and ENP. A specific feature of the language of the *Qorān-e-Qods* is the frequent usage of old agent nouns in -*dār/-tār* suffixed to the past stem (and merged with a stem-final -*d*), translating Arabic active participles, e.g., '*šīr-dādār* =milk-giving'[1]. Only the verb 'do' uses the present stem here with the suffix -*ār* (e.g., '*ḥesāb-konārān* =(those) who count'[2], showing that forms like *dādār* were probably understood as *dād-ār*. These agent nouns are sometimes combined with forms of the verb 'to be' to translate full verbs, e.g., '*budim āzemudārān* =we have examined'[3].

Particles: Prepositions play an important grammatical role in Middle Persian and Early stage of New Persian, because they have taken over most case functions after

---

[1] Ravāqi, 1984: p. 211.

[2] Ravāqi, 1984: p. 208.

[3] Ravāqi, 1984: p. 220; please also see: Filippone, 2011: pp. 195-96.

the loss of the nominal inflectional system of Old Persian. Certain prepositions of this stage show a transitory stage formally from Middle Persian to (later) New Persian; e.g., '(a)bar =upon', '(an)dar =in', 'furō(δ) =down to' of the ENP; cf. Middle Persian *abar* (later *bar*), *andar* (later *dar*), *furōd* (later *furō* then *foru*). The function of certain ENP prepositions is straightforward and quite stable from Middle Persian to Early stage of New Persian and beyond, e.g., '*az* =from' or '*(an)dar* =in'.

That of others is more complex and difficult to describe, e.g., the ENP preposition '*abā(z)* =back to', which is derived from the two separate prepositions of '*abāz* =later *bāz*', and '*abāy* =with' of the Middle Persian and has retained the corresponding two separate meanings of 'back to' and 'with', which cannot always be clearly separated[1].

---

[1] Lazard, 1963: p. 680.

Allophonic Variation:

In Modern Persian, the voiceless obstruents /p, t, tʃ, k/ are aspirated much like their English counterparts; they become aspirated when they begin a syllable, though aspiration is not contrastive[1]. Persian does not have syllable-initial consonant clusters so, unlike in English, /p, t, k/ are aspirated even following /s/, as in هستم /hæstæm/ ('I exist')[2].

They are also aspirated at the end of syllables, although not as strongly. In some dialects and accents the stops /k, g/ are palatalized before front vowels or at the end of a syllable. In Classical Persian, (/ɣ/ غ) and (/ɢ/ ق) denoted the original Arabic phonemes. In Modern Persian (which is used in the Iranian mass media, both colloquial and standard) there is no difference in the pronunciation of the letter (/ɣ/ غ) and the letter (/ɢ/ ق), and they are both normally pronounced as a voiced uvular stop [ɢ]. The classic pronunciations of (/ɣ/ غ) and (/ɢ/ ق) are preserved in the eastern varieties, Dari and Tajiki, as well as in the southern varieties.

The alveolar flap /ɾ/ has a trilled allophonic variant [r] at the beginning of a word, a free variation between a trill [r] and a flap [ɾ][3]; the trill [r] as a separate phoneme occurs word-medially especially in loanwords of Arabic origin as a result of gemination of [ɾ]. An alveolar approximant [ɹ] also occurs as an allophone of /ɾ/ before /t, d, s, z, ʃ, l/ and /ʒ/; [ɹ] is sometimes in free variation with [ɾ] in these and other positions, such that

---

[1] Mahootian, 1997: pp. 287, 292, 303, 305.
[2] Mace (1993).
[3] Mahootian, 1997: pp. 287, 292, 303, 305.

is pronounced [fɒːɹsiː] or [fɒːrsiː], /r/ is sometimes realized as a long approximant [ɹː]. The velar nasal [ŋ] is an allophone of /n/ before /k, g/; /f, k, s, ʃ, x/ may be voiced to, respectively, [v, g, z, ʒ, ɣ] before voiced consonants; /n/ may be bilabial [m] before bilabial consonants. Also /b/ may in some cases change into [β], or even [v], for example باز ('open') may be pronounced [bɒːz] as well as [vɒːz] or [vɒː], colloquially.

Dialectal Variation: The pronunciation of [w و] in Classical Persian shifted to [v] in (Iranian) Modern Persian, but is retained in Dari and in some dialects of Tajiki. In Modern Persian [w] is lost if preceded by a consonant and followed by a vowel in one whole syllable, e.g. /x(w)ɒːb/[1], as Persian has no syllable-initial consonant clusters.

Consonants can be geminated, often in words from Arabic. This is represented in the IPA either by doubling the consonant, [səjjəd], or with the length marker ⟨ː⟩, [səjːəd][2].

---

[1] 'sleep' (خواب)

[2] Vrzić, 2007: p. xxiii.

Phonotactics

Syllable structure: In Modern Persian, syllables may be structured as (C)(S)V(S)(C(C)[1&2].

Modern Persian syllable structure consists of an optional syllable onset, consisting of one consonant; an obligatory syllable nucleus, consisting of a vowel optionally preceded by and/or followed by a semivowel; and an optional syllable coda, consisting of one or two consonants. The following restrictions apply:

- Onset

- Consonant (C): Can be any consonant. (Onset is composed only of one consonant; consonant clusters are only found in loanwords, sometimes an epenthetic /æ/ is inserted between consonants.)

- Nucleus

- Semivowel (S)

- Vowel (V)

- Semivowel (S)

- Coda

- First consonant (C): Can be any consonant.

- Second consonant (C): Can also be any consonant (mostly /d/, /k/, /s/, /t/, & /z/).

---

[1] Mahootian, 1997: pp. 287, 292, 303, 305.
[2] Jahani, 2005: pp. 79–96.

Word Accent: In Modern Persian word-accent is described as a stress accent and as a pitch accent[1], and the accented syllables are generally pronounced with a raised pitch as well as stress; but in certain contexts words may become unaccented and lose their high pitch[2&3]. From an intonational aspect, Persian words (or accentual phrases) usually have the intonation (L +) H*[4]: /kətɒːb/'book' (کتاب); unless there is a suffix, in which case the intonation is (L+) H*+L: /kətɒːbæm/'my book' (کتابم). The last accent of a sentence is usually accompanied by a low boundary tone, which produces a falling pitch on the last accented syllable, e.g. /ɒːn kətɒːb buːd/[5]. If two words are joined in an *ezafe* construction, they can either be pronounced accentually as two separate words, e.g. /mærdom ə iːndʒɒː/[6], or else the first word loses its high tone and the two words are pronounced as a single accentual phrase: /mærdom ə iːndʒɒː/. Words also become unaccented following a focused word; for example, in the sentence /nɒːmə jə mɒːmɒːnæm ruːjə miːz buːd/[7] all the syllables following the word /mɒːmɒːn/ 'mom' (مامان)- are pronounced with a low pitch[8]. Knowing the rules for the correct placement of the accent is essential for proper pronunciation[9].

---

[1] Abolhasanizadeh, & Others (2012).

[2] Sadat-Tehrani, 2007; pp.3, 22, 46-47, 51.

[3] Hosseini, 2014: pp.22f, 35.

[4] L is low and H* is a high-toned stressed syllable.

[5] 'it was a book' (آن کتاب بود)

[6] 'the people (of) here' (مردم اینجا)

[7] 'it was my mom's letter on the table' (نامۀ مامانم روی میز بود)

[8] Sadat-Tehrani, 2007: pp.3, 22, 46-47, 51.

[9] Mace (2003).

Colloquial Modern Persian: When spoken formally, Modern Persian is pronounced as written. But colloquial pronunciation as used by all classes makes a number of very common substitutions. Note that Iranians can interchange colloquial and formal sociolects in conversational speech; they include[1]: In the Tehrâni accent and also most of the accents in Central and Southern Iran, the sequence /ɒːn/ in the colloquial language is nearly always pronounced [un]. The only common exceptions are high prestige words, such as [ʔiːrɒːn][2], and foreign nouns (both common and proper), like the Spanish surname [bəltrɒːn][3], which are pronounced as written. A few words written as /ɒːn/ are pronounced [uːn], especially forms like /təhrɒːn/ which may become /təhruːn/. In the Tehrâni accent, the unstressed direct object suffix marker /rɒː/ is pronounced /ro/ after a vowel, and /o/ after a consonant. The 2ⁿᵈ and 3ʳᵈ person plural verb subject suffixes, written /-iːd/ and /-ænd/ respectively, are pronounced [-iːn] and [-æn]. The stems of many frequently-occurring verbs have a short colloquial form, especially /æst/[4], which is colloquially shortened to /e/ after a consonant or /s/ after a vowel. Also, the stems of verbs which end in /h/ and /v/ or a vowel are shortened; e.g:

می‌خواهم /'miːxɒːhæm/ ('I want') → ['miːxɒːm],

می‌روم /'miɾævæm/ ('I go') → ['miːɾæm].

---

[1] Thackston, 1993: pp. 205–214.

[2] 'Iran' (ایران)

[3] 'Betran' (بلتران)

[4] 'he/she is' (است)

The Urdu Language

Urdu, the national language of Pakistan is the most important language of literacy, literature, office and court business, media and religious institutions of Pakistan. Urdu is taught from primary to intermediate level as a compulsory subject and as an optional subject at degree level in Pakistan. At Intermediate and degree level most of the students of Humanities and Social Sciences choose Urdu as a medium of education. Urdu is not an indigenous language in Pakistan and suffers from a lot of pressures of different ethnic and linguistic groups.

Historical Introduction of the Urdu Usage: There are many assumptions pertaining to the origin of Urdu, differing in both time and geographic location. Urdu is an Indo-European language originated in India, most likely in Delhi, from where it spread to the rest of the subcontinent. Other major metropolitan areas with a strong tradition of the language include Hyderabad, Lukhnow and Lahore. Another view is that the Urdu language was originated during the Mughal period (1526-1858), and it was borne out of the socio-administrative needs of Muslim rulers. It literally means "a camp language", "troops", or "army" for it was spoken by the troops of Mughal Empire when the soldiers from Central mixed with the speakers of local dialects of Northern India. When the Mughal army constituted by king Babar, it included the soldiers from all over the regions of South Asia and the surrounding states like Iran, Afghanistan, Arab, Russia and Turkey. Hence an amalgamation of all the spoken languages resulted in the formulation of Urdu. Initially it was emerged as a synthesis of Khari

Boli (Hindi), Braj Bhasha Rajhistani and Punjabi with some Arabic and Persian vocabulary. During the first two centuries of its development, i.e. during the thirteenth and fourteenth centuries, "Urdu, cutting across the regional barriers'[1] not only became popular far and wide but also spread and developed linguistically. Thus, Urdu became a lingua franca or link language for communications between the troops from foreign lands and the native people. "The lingua franca, with the continuous deployment of armies to South India, eventually got established in the Muslim kingdoms of the South: there it was known under the name Dakni, (Daccan = South)"[2]. Like all other languages, Urdu had to go through the stages of evolution and development. New words were created that belonged only to the Urdu language. Urdu began to become famous because of its flexible nature to absorb the words from other languages. Increasingly, words and grammatical structure of Persian, the official language of the Mughal administrators, were incorporated until Urdu attained its stylized, literary form in the seventeenth and eighteenth centuries. Urdu has always been written using the Persian script. Urdu has a history of more than 700 years. But its character set was not standardized till January 26, 2004[3]. Looking back to the history of the evolution of Urdu language from its birth during the Mughal period 1526 to 1905, the long period can be divided into three stages.

---

[1] Beg, 1996: p. 40.
[2] Pandit, 1977: p. 57.
[3] Platts (2005).

Stage 1 (1526 to 1707): The kingdom of Mughals started with the throne of Babar in 1526 but moved towards the south when Aurangzeb was died in 1707. "The word 'Urdu' is a Turkish word that stands for a "military language" or "horde""[1]. Urdu had not taken its complete form in this era. It was actually the mixture of the dialects spoken by the Muslims who had been ruling over the South Asia from 14th century. "The form of the language as a result of mixing various dialects was known as Dakhni or the speech of the South may be traced back to the 15th century"[2] (Kashmiri 2003). Its use was confined only to Daccan and South India and was used in literature by the Muslims of these regions, who were less influenced by the local Hindi spirit of the dialects and languages of North India than the Muslims living in North India. This difference becomes quite clear from the fact that the Perso-Arabic script was used in the Daccan from almost the beginning. Gradually, the literature increasingly came under foreign influence in the sense that it became more and more Muslim and Persian in its attitude and attributes Urdu, however, continued to adopt and use a great collection from Indian vocabulary till the end of the 17th century[3].

Stage 2 (1707 to 1815): This era commenced when Aurangzeb died in 1707 and ended with the third Maratha war in 1818 and Urdu was brought forth as a language during this period. "Delhi and Lukhnow were the two central places which received much influence of

---

[1] Nayyer (2003), in: Ashraf, 1975: p. 30.
[2] Kashmiri (2003).
[3] Nayyer (2003), in: Ashraf, 1975: p. 30.

the development of Urdu"[1]. There was a significant contribution of both Arabic and Persian languages seen in the development and expansion of Urdu. A strong need for the rehabilitation of the ethical and socio economic condition was felt when the situation in the Muslim society became worse due to the weaknesses in the royal authorities. "The Muslim scholars decided upon brining the Muslim community together by reforming the society on religious grounds. Arabic was considered to be the channel to meet the needs of religious rethinking among the Muslims"[2]. The Muslim society was agreed upon a thought to adopt a language that would show their linguistic identity and Urdu served this purpose quite successfully in the 18th century. By 1750, Delhi Urdu entered upon its new and triumphant career and helped to establish the Hindustani Speech all over India. When the British came to India, they realized the need to communicate in Urdu, which is why they set up an Urdu center at the Fort William College in Calcutta to teach British employees the language. The college helped promote Urdu too.

Stage 3 (1815 to 1905): During 1815 to 1905, Urdu was flourished as a language of communication. A major development during this era was that Urdu was introduced as a language of literature. "The language which was born in the camps of military troops from the Hindi Khari/Khadi Boli during the later Mughal period, developed into a language of expression for religious and philosophic ideology"[3]. An Urdu translation of the Holy

---

[1] Nayyer (2003), in: Ashraf, 1975: p. 31.
[2] Beg (1996).
[3] Nayyer (2003), in: Ashraf, 1975: p. 31.

Quran was made in 1791. It was during this period that Urdu became popular as a spoken language and replaced Persian as the language of the educated people. During this period, Lukhnow and Rampur were the centers of Urdu. The Aligarh Movement promoted to modernize Urdu literature at the beginning of the fourth quarter of the 19th century. It was just because of the Aligarh movement that a large number of prose writers, historians and essayists contributed their share to the Urdu literature. "With the passage of time, Urdu became to be regarded as the language of the Muslims"[1]. Muslim leadership demanded before the Hunter Commission (between 1883 to 1890) in Bengal that special and urgent step should be taken for the primary education of Hindus and Muslims. They stressed that Urdu should be made the medium of instruction in education. During these years, Urdu press was launched and the books and reading material started to be published. As Indian Muslim started identifying themselves with this language and Urdu was regarded as the language of the Muslims, it became a bone of contention between the Muslims and the Hindus.

Educational Policies with Special Reference to Urdu: When Pakistan was emerged on the face of the world, its main demand was to satisfy the two conflicting requirements of 'nationism' and 'nationalism'[2]. The urge of nationalism was satisfied by declaring Urdu as the national language and a sign to unite the masses of the new country. "An appropriate status for Bengali, that was the language of the East Pakistan, was demanded

---

[1] Kashmiri (2003).
[2] Bell, 1976: pp. 168-9.

that proved a sense of resentment on declaring Urdu as the only national language"[1]. After the Dacca language riots the politicians suggested that there could be only one lingua franca or a link language in order to link the people of different provinces of the country and that language should be Urdu[2]. With the rooted policy of decreasing the importance and usage of Prsian language, English filled in the need for 'nationism', which was the requirement of the new government officials to start the machinery of the state at operational level. Therefore, English was decided to be the official language.

A Movement for the Promotion of Urdu: The policy that was made by adopting English as an official language, the language of British rulers, and an attempt to maintain the balance of status between English and Urdu was soon criticized and pressurized by those who were the protagonists of promoting Urdu. They demand a policy in which English would totally be replaced by Urdu in official use. Efforts to abandon English to replace it with Urdu have been a consistent and continuous policy of the government for the tools used by almost all the governments to achieve this purpose of national unity were to gain authentic control of the syllabus, curriculum and the use of Urdu as a medium of instruction in the educational system. All these efforts were made to strengthen Urdu so that government could make it sure that a uniform policy has been implemented throughout the state. Tthe emergence and construction of a new system of education, however, was the only one reason and rationale to convince the people on the

---

[1] Mansoor, 1993.
[2] Haque, 1982: p. 6.

subject of national unity[1]. Urdu, which is not an indigenous language to Pakistan, came to occupy the position of the national language of Pakistan and the most commonly used medium of instruction in government schools. According to the Census of 1951: Urdu is the normal medium of instruction in primary and middle schools in West Pakistan except where instruction is given in Sindhi, Pushto or English and even there Urdu is taught as the second language. In West Pakistan therefore as a general rule most people who can write at all, write Urdu[2].

---

[1] Mansoor (1993).
[2] Rahman, 1997: p. 146.

Vowels: As it is shown in the above table, Urdu does not have short vowels at the end of words, the following table is a comprehensive chart to represent 10 vowels:

Romanization	Pronunciation	Final Form	Middle Form	Initial Form	Isolated Form
a	/ə/	ویژہ	سیر	اندر	اِ
ā	/aː/	وفا	باغ	آم	آ
i	/ɪ/		دن	دوسر	اِ
ī	/iː/	گھمڑی	تیسرا	اینٹ	ای
e	/ə/	دریگے	میرا	ایک	اے
ai	/ɛː/	ہے	کیِسا	ایسا	اَے
u	/ʊ/		سلطان	الفت	اُ
ū	/uː/	قابو	دور	اوپر	او
o	/oː/	کو	دوست	اوس	او
au	/ɔː/	نو	موسم	اور	او

92

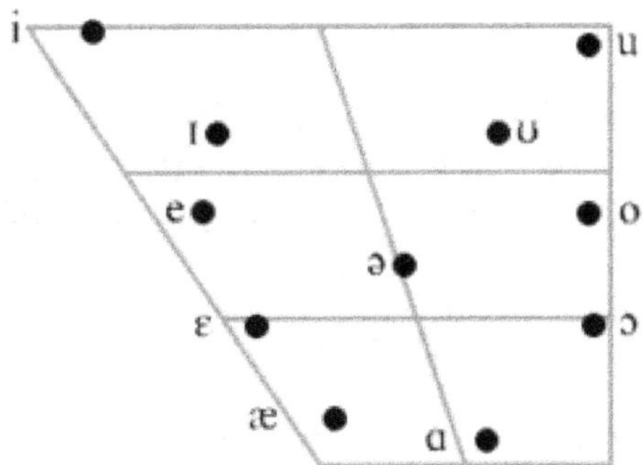

The oral vowel phonemes of Hindi according to Ohala
(1999:102)[1]

Besides the 10 vowels **Urdu** has 10 nasalized vowels. Each vowel has four forms depending on its position: initial, middle, final and isolated. Like in its parent Perso-Arabic alphabet, Urdu vowels are represented using a combination of digraphs and diacritics. Alif, Waw, Ye, He and their variants are used to represent vowels.

Important Notes: *Alif, Wā'o, Ye, He, Ayn, Nun Ghunnah, Hamza, Iẓāfat*

Vowel: Urdu doesn't have standalone vowel letters. Short vowels *(a, i, u)* are represented by optional diacritics *(zabar, zer, pesh)* upon the preceding consonant or a placeholder consonant *(alif, ain, or hamzah)* if the syllable begins with the vowel, and long vowels by consonants *alif, ain, ye,* and *wa'o* as

---

[1] Ohala's chart represent the Hindi vowels.

matres lectionis[1], with disambiguating diacritics, some of which are optional *(zabar, zer, pesh)*, whereas some are not *(madd, hamzah)*.

alif: Alif is the first letter of the Urdu alphabet, and it is used exclusively as a vowel. At the beginning of a word, alif can be used to represent any of the short vowels: اب ab, اسم ism, اردو Urdū. For long ā at the beginning of words: آپ /ɒːp/, but a plain alif in the middle and at the end: بھاگنا /bhɒːgnɒː/.

Wāʾo: Wāʾo is used to render the vowels "ū" to represent [uː], "o", to represent [oː], "u" to represent [ʊ], and "au" to represent [ɔː] respectively, and it is also used to render the labiodental approximant: [ʋ].

Ye: Ye is divided into two variants: *choṭī ye* "little ye" -ی- and *baṛī ye* "big ye" -ے-.

Choṭī ye (ی) is written in all forms exactly as in Persian. It is used for the long vowel "ī" and the consonant "y".

Baṛī ye (ے) is used to render the vowels "e" and "ai" (/ə/ and /ɛː/ respectively). *Baṛī ye* is distinguishable in

---

[1] In the spelling of some languages, matres lectionis (English: /ˈmeɪtriːz lɛktiˈoʊnɪs/; from Latin "mothers of reading") refers to the use of certain consonants to indicate a vowel.

writing from *choṭī ye* only when it comes at the end of a word/ligature. Additionally, *Baṛī ye* is never used to begin a word/ligature, unlike *choṭī ye*.

The 2 he's: *'he'* is divided into two variants: *choṭī he* (little he - ہ -) is written zigzagged as it can only be

used as in Persian, and *do-cashmī he* (two-eyed he - ھ)

which is written in all forms exactly as in Arabic Naskh style (as a loop), in order to create the aspirate consonants.

Letter's name	Final Form	Middle Form	Initial Form	Isolated Form
چھوٹی یے choṭī ye	ی	ﻴ	ﻳ	ی
بڑی یے baṛī ye	ے			ے
چھوٹی ہے choṭī he	ﻪ	ﻬ	ﻫ ہ	ہ
دو چشمی ہے do-cashmī he	ﻪ	ﻬ	ﻬ	ھ

Ayn: *Ayn* in its initial and final position is silent in pronunciation and is replaced by the sound of its preceding or succeeding vowel.

Nun Ghunnah: Nasalized vowels are represented by Nun Ghunnah written after their non nasalized versions. like for example ـے when nasalized would become ہیں. In middle form Nun Gunnah is written just like Nun and is differentiated by a diacritic called Maghnoona or Ulta Jazm which is a superscript V symbol above the ں.

Form	Urdu	Transcription
Orthography	ں	n̲
End Form	میں	main̲
Middle Form	کنول	kan̲wal

Hamza: In Urdu, Hamza is silent in all its forms except for when it is used as Hamza-e-Izafat. The main use of Hamza in Urdu is to indicate a vowel cluster.

Iẓāfat: Iẓāfat is a syntactical construction of two nouns, where the first component is a determined noun, and the second is a determiner. This construction was borrowed from Persian. A short vowel "i" is used to connect these two words. It may be written as *zer* (ِ) at the end of the first word, but usually it is not written at all. If the first word ends in *choṭī he* (ہ) or *choṭī ye* (ی), then *hamzā* (ء) is used above the last letter (ۂ or ئ). If the first word ends in a long vowel then *baṛī ye* (ے) with *hamzā* on top (ۓ) is written[1].

Diacritics: Urdu is normally written only with letters, diacritics being optional. However, the letters represent just the consonantal content of the string and in some cases (under-specified) vocalic content. The vocalic content may be optionally or completely specified by using diacritics with the letters[2]. Hence, Urdu uses the same subset of diacritics used in Arabic based on Persian conventions. Urdu also uses Persian names of the diacritics instead of Arabic names. Commonly used diacritics are Zabar (Arabic Fatḥah), Zer (Arabic Kasrah), Pesh (Arabic Ḍammah) which are used to clarify the pronunciation of vowels. Jazam (Arabic Sukun) is used to indicate a Consonant Cluster and Shadd (Arabic Tashdid) which is used to indicate a Gemination. Other diacritics include Khari Zabar (Arabic Dagger alif), Do Zabar (Arabic Fathatan) which are found in some common Arabic loan words. Other Arabic diacritics are also sometimes used though very rarely in loan words

---

[1] Delacy, 2003: p. 99–100.
[2] Hussain (2004).

from Arabic. Other than common diacritics, Urdu also has special diacritics, which are often found only in dictionaries for the clarification of irregular pronunciation. These diacritics include Kasrah-e-Majhool, Fathah-e-Majhool, Dammah-e-Majhool, Maghnoona[1], Ulta Jazam, Alif-e-Wavi and some other very rare diacritics.

Other diacritics are only rarely written in printed form mainly in some advance dictionaries[2]. Two characters (marks) of Urdu are part of Urdu Zabita Takhti[3] but not present in Unicode[4]. There is at least one mark and one character of Urdu, written in books and dictionaries, which is neither part of UZT, nor of Unicode. However, the variants of these characters as well as the marks are not standardized by any body or authority yet. No complete, (almost error free) dictionary, corpus or lexicon of Urdu with correct marks has yet been prepared using Unicode. Some serious efforts, including a few sponsored, have been made for preparation of computerized Urdu dictionaries, however, none is comparable with any standard/printed one. Among several causes of the flaw, one is absence of the certain marks that are used for producing proper pronunciation. Similarly, text-tospeech systems cannot produce correct sound till they are trained with correct marks for any sound. After reviewing several dictionaries, it is observed that without inclusion of these three symbols,

---

[1] Among these, only Maghnoona is used commonly in dictionaries and has a unicode representation at u0658.

[2] Numan (2009).

[3] UZT (1.01)

[4] 5.1.0

development of a correct dictionary and a text-to-speech system for Urdu is not possible, Numan (2009) in his research "Proposal of Inclusion of Certain Characters in Unicode" surveyed the subject[1].

Consonants (Persian alphabet and Urdu):

Urdu has more letters added to the Persian base to represent sounds not present in Persian, which already has additional letters added to the Arabic base itself to represent sounds not present in Arabic:

ٹ to represent /ʈ/

ڈ to represent /ɖ/

ڑ to represent /ɽ/

ں to represent /õ/

ے to represent /ɛ:/ or /e:/

Furthermore, a separate do-cashmi-he letter, ھ, exists to denote a /ʰ/ or a /ɦ/. This letter is mainly used as part of the multitude of digraphs, detailed below. Urdu writings is in Perso-Arabic script in Nastaleeq style using an extended Arabic character set. The character set includes basic and secondary letters, aerab (or diacritical marks), punctuation marks and special symbols.

Urdu script: The Urdu script is an abjad script derived from Perso-Arabic script, which is itself a derivative of the Arabic script. The Urdu alphabet was standardized in 2004 by the National Language Authority, which is responsible for standardizing Urdu in Pakistan. According to the National Language Authority, Urdu has

---

[1] For more information please refer to the main source: Numan (2009).

58 letters of which 39 are basic letters while 18 are digraphs to represent aspirated consonants made by attaching basic consonant letters with a variant of *He* called *do chashmi he*[1]. Tā' marbūṭah is also sometimes considered a letter though it is rarely used except for in certain loan words from Arabic. As an abjad, the Urdu script only shows consonants and long vowels; short vowels can only be inferred by the consonants' relation to each other. While this type of script is convenient in Semitic languages like Arabic and Hebrew, whose consonant roots are the key of the sentence.

Urdu Spelling: In Urdu, there is no concept of capitalization. Proper names cannot be identified through script analysis and there is no 'Urdu specific' algorithm for named entity tagging. Spelling variations are quite common in Urdu. The main reason for these variations is that there are many homophone characters (different letters representing the same phoneme) in Urdu. Also people tend to confuse different homophones for each other, so, as a result, incorrect spelling of words having homophones becomes quite common.

For example, 'ز' and 'ذ' are homophone characters and are very frequently confused with each other. The word 'پذیر' /pæzi:r/ is commonly written in news papers, books and some dictionaries with letter 'ز' instead of 'ذ' which is considered as being correct. Urdu collation sequence is fully standardized. In Urdu, three levels of sorting are required for letters, diacritics and special symbols[2].

---

[1] Ijaz | Hussain.

[2] Ijaz | Hussain, p. 2.

CATALOUGUE

of

PERSIAN

AND

URDU

PROVERBS

Urdu	Persian
آپ زنده، جہاں زنده ـ آپ مرده، جہاں مرده /ɒːp zindæ d͡ʒæhɒːn zindæ - ɒːp mordæ d͡ʒæhɒːn mordæ/ *Morovvat, 2007:1.* معنای برابر فارسی)= خود زنده، جهان زنده ـ خود مرده، جهان (مرده Persian Equivalent Meaning: /χod zəndə, d͡ʒæhɒːn zəndə – χod mordə, d͡ʒæhɒːn mordə/	مشابه: **دیگی که برای من نجوشد، سر** **سگ در آن بجوشد** Equivalent: /diːgiː kə bærɒːjə mæn næd͡ʒuːʃæd særə sæg dær ɒːn bəd͡ʒuːʃæd/ *Dehkhoda, 1984: 850.*

Proverb's English equivalent: ***After us the deluge***

1877 HENRY GEORGE *The Ode to Liberty* Is it a light thing that labor should be robbed of its earnings while greed rolls in wealth -- that the many should want while the few are surfeited? Turn to history, and on every page may be read the lesson that such wrong never goes unpunished; that the Nemesis that follows injustice never falters nor sleeps! Look around to-day. Can this state of things continue? May we even say, "After us the deluge!" Nay; the pillars of the state are trembling even now, and the very foundations of society begin to quiver with pent-up forces that glow underneath.

The struggle that must either revivify, or convulse in ruin, is near at hand, if it be not already begun.

1898 E. COBHAM BREWER *Dictionary of Phrase and Fable* "I care not what happens when I am dead and gone." So said Mdme. de Pompadour, the mistress of Louis XV. (*1722–1764*). Metternich, the Austrian statesman (*1773–1859*), is credited with the same: but probably he simply quoted the words of the French marchioness.

Urdu	Persian

آپ کو فصیحت اور کو نصیحت

ɒːp ko fæsiːhæt or ko/
/ næsiːhæt

.Morovvat, 2007:1

(معنای برابر فارسی= خود را
فصیحت، دیگران را نصیحت)

Persian Equivalent Meaning:

/χod ɒː fæsiːhæt, digærɒːn
ɒː næsiːhæt/

مشابه:

کور خود است و بینای مردم

Equivalent:

/kuːr ə χod æst o biːnɒːjə
mærdom/

Dehkhoda, 1984: 1243.

Proverb's English equivalent: *Judge not, that ye be not judged*

1481 CAXTON *Reynard* (**1880**) xxix. Deme1 ye noman, and ye shal not be demed.

1509 H. WATSON *Ship of Fools* H1 Judge not but yf that ye wyl be juged.

1925 A. CLUTTON–BROCK *Essays on Life* x. The saying, Judge not, that ye be not judged,' is... a statement of fact. Nothing makes us dislike a man so much as the knowledge that he is always judging us and all men.

1979 C. DEXTER *Service of all Dead* i. 'Judge not- that ye be not judged.' Judge not- at least until the evidence is unequivocal.

---

[1] judge

Urdu	Persian

آپ کا نوکر ہوں، بینگنوں کا نوکر نہیں

/ɒ:p kɒ: nokær hu:n bi:ngu:n kɒ: nokær nəhi:n/

Morovvat, 2007:2.

(معنای برابر فارسی= من نوکر حاکمم نه نوکر بادمجان)

Persian Equivalent Meaning:

/mæn nokær ə hɒ:kəmæm næ nokær ə bɒ:dəndʒɒ:n/

بادنجان باد دارد بلی ندارد بلی

/bɒ:dəndʒɒ:n bɒ:d dɒ:ræd bæli: nædɒ:ræd bæli:/

مشابه:

بوجار لنجان است هر سو باد می‌آید باد می‌دهد

Equivalent:

/bu:dʒɒ:r ə ləndʒɒ:n æst hær su: bɒ:d mi ɒ:jæd bɒ:d mi: dæhæd/

Dehkhoda, 1984: 470.

Proverb's English equivalent: ***Like master, like man***

1530 J. PALSGRAVE *L'éclaircissement de la Langue Française* **120**[v] Suche maystre such man.[1]

1538 ELYOT *Dict.* s.v. Similes, A lewde[2] servaunt with an yll master … Lyke master lyke man.

1620 T. SHELTON tr. *Cervantes' Don Quixote* II. x. The Prouerbe be true that sayes, like master, like man',and I may add, 'like lady, like maid'. Lady Hercules was fine, but her maid was still finer.

---

[1] servant
[2] ill–mannered, foolish

1979 M. G. EBERHART *Bayou Road* iv. 'Like master, like man,' Marcy's father had said bitterly ... of the disappearance of an entire set of Dresden plates.

Proverb's English equivalent: *Like lady, like maid*

1724 DANIEL DEFOE *Roxana (Essays on Roxana)* And as Susan becomes a threat to her social security, Roxana perceives no other means to get rid of her daughter than to murder her, with the help and meditation of Amy ... The only social link she maintains throughout the novel is the link that which binds her to her servant Amy, as they share the same fate (for instance, Amy and the Prince's man mimic Roxana and the Prince), as well as the same passions : "like Mistress, like Maid".

1840 FREDERICK MARRYAT *Poor Jack* Volume X Chapter 1 But I must now introduce a more important personage than even Lady Hercules, which is my mother. They say "like master, like man," and I may add, "like lady, like maid." Lady Hercules was fine, but her maid was still finer ...

2003 JENNIFER SPEAKE *The Oxford Dictionary of Proverbs* Like Master, Like Man, Man here is in the sense of 'servant'. The female equivalent is like mistress like maid. Cf. Petronius Satyricon lviii. qualis dominus , talis et servus , as is the master, so is the servant; early 14th-cent. Fr. lon dit a tel seigneur tel varlet, it is said, for such a lord such a manservant. 1530 J. Palsgrave L'éclaircissement de la Langue Française 120^V Suche maystre suche man. 1538 T. Elyot Dict. s.v. Similes, A lewde [foolish] servaunt with an yll master ... Lyke master lyke man. 1620 T. Shelton tr. Cervantes' Don Quixote.

<table>
<thead>
<tr><th style="text-align:center">Urdu</th><th style="text-align:center">Persian</th></tr>
</thead>
<tbody>
<tr>
<td>آج کا کام کل پر مت ٹالو
/ɒːd͡ʒ kɒ: kæm pær mat tɒ:lo/
Morovvat, 2007:2.</td>
<td>کار امروز بفردا مفکن
/kɒ:r ə əmruz bə færdɒ: mæfəkæn/
Dehkhoda, 1984: 1172.</td>
</tr>
</tbody>
</table>

Proverb's English equivalent: ***Delays are dangerous***

[*c* **1300** *Havelok* (**1915**) l. **1352** Dwelling haueth ofte scathe1 wrouth.]

1578 LYLY *Euphues* I. **212** Delayes breed daungers, nothing so perillous as procrastination.

1655 J. SHIRLEY *Gentlemen of Venice* v. **62** Shall we go presently,2 delaies are dangerous.

1824 J. FAIRFIELD *Letters* (**1922**) p. xxxi, I have always found on all subjects that 'delays are dangerous' ... It is expedient that we marry young.

1930 B. FLYNN *Murder en Route* xxxiii. What a pity Master Hector left it too late ... Delays are proverbially dangerous.

---

[1] harm, damage
[2] immediately (archaic)

Urdu	Persian
آگ اور بیری کو کم نہ سمجھے	آتش اگر اندک است حقیر نباید داشت
ɒ̃ːg or biːriː ko kæm nə sam/ / dʒhiː	/ɒːtæʃ ægær ændæk æst hæGiːr næbɒːjæd dɒːʃt/
.Morovvat, 2007:2	*Dehkhoda, 1984: 16.*
(معنای برابر فارسی= آب و آتش را حقیر مشمار)	
Persian Equivalent Meaning:	
/ɒːb o ɒːtæʃ rɒː hæGiːr mæʃmɒːr/	

Proverb's English equivalent: ***Even a worm will turn***

1546 J. HEYWOOD *Dialogue of Proverbs* II. iv. G4ᵛ Treade a worme on the tayle, & it must turne agayne.

1592 GREENE *Groatsworth of Wit* XII. **143** Stop shallow water still running, it will rage. Tread on a worme and it will turne.

1854 M. LANGDON *Ida* May xi. Even the worm turns when he is trodden upon.

1889 W. JAMES in *Mind* XIV. **107** Since even the worm will 'turn', the space–theorist can hardly be expected to remain motionless when his Editor stirs him up.

1962 A. CHRISTIE *Mirror Crack'd* xii. He's a very meek type. Still, the worm will turn, or so they say.

1967 RIDOUT & WITTING *English Proverbs Explained* *52* 'This morning that cantankerous wife of his tried to pick a quarrel with the conductor, and Percy told her ... to shut up.' 'Good for Percy! Even a worm will turn.'

W. SHAKESPEAR – *Henry* IV:

Clifford: *My gracious liege, this too much lenity*

And harmful pity must be laid aside.

To whom do lions cast their gentle looks?

Not to the beast that would usurp their den.

Whose hand is that the forest bear doth lick?

Not his that spoils her young before her face.

Who 'scapes the lurking serpent's mortal sting?

Not he that sets his foot upon her back.

The smallest worm will turn being trodden on,

And doves will peck in safeguard of their brood.

Urdu	Persian
آگ اور پانی کا سنجوگ	آب و آتش به هم نیاید راست
/ɒːg or pɒːniː kɒː sændʒuːg/	
Morovvat, 2007:2.	/ɒːb o ɒːtæʃ bə hæm næjɒːjæd rɒːst/
(معنای برابر فارسی= آب و آتش را چه آشنایی)	Dehkhoda, 1984: 14.
Persian Equivalent Meaning:	
/ɒːb o ɒːtæʃ rɒː t͡ʃæ ɒːʃænɒːiː/	

Proverb's English equivalent: *You can't put new wine in old bottles*

The English resemble has its root in the Bible: *[Neither doe men put new wine into old bottles: else the bottles breake, and the wine runneth out, and the bottles perish]* Matthew ix. 17.

1912 L. STRACHEY *Landmarks in French Literature* vi. The new spirits had animated the prose of Chateaubriand and the poetry of Lamartine; but ... the *form* of both these writers retained most of the important characteristics of the old tradition. It was new wine in old bottles.

1948 A. J. TYNBEE *Civilization on Trial* vi. The new wines of industrialism and democracy have been poured into old bottles and they have burst the old bottles beyond repair.

1960 I. JEFFERIES *Dignity & Purity* viii. 'I don't think you can put new wine in old bottles.' I looked doubtful ... 'A lot of this could be rationalized.'

1979 T. SHARPE *Porter-house Blue* x.'Motives? ... Good old fashioned lust.' 'That hardly explains the explosive nature of his end.' ... 'You can't put new wine in old bottles.'

Urdu	Persian
آگ و پانی کا بیر ہے	آب و آتش به هم نیاید راست
/ɒːg o pɒːniː kɒː biːr hə/	/ɒːb o ɒːtæʃ bə hæm næjɒːjæd rɒːst/
Morovvat, 2007:2.	*Dehkhoda, 1984: 14.*
(معنای برابر فارسی= آب و آتش خلاف یکدگرند)	

Persian Equivalent Meaning:

/ɒːb o ɒːtæʃ χælɒːfə jədəgærænd/

Proverb's English equivalent: *You can't put new wine in old bottles*

1912 L. STRACHEY *Landmarks in French Literature* vi. The new spirits had animated the prose of Chateaubriand and the poetry of Lamartine; but … the form of both these writers retained most of the important characteristics of the old tradition. It was new wine in old bottles.

1948 A. J. TYNBEE *Civilization on Trial* vi. The new wines of industrialism and democracy have been poured into old bottles and they have burst the old bottles beyond repair.

1960 I. JEFFERIES *Dignity & Purity* viii. 'I don't think you can put new wine in old bottles.' I looked doubtful … 'A lot of this could be rationalized.'

1979 T. SHARPE *Porter-house Blue* x.'Motives? … Good old fashioned lust.' 'That hardly explains the explosive nature of his end.' … 'You can't put new wine in old bottles.'

<table>
<tr><td align="center">Urdu</td><td align="center">Persian</td></tr>
</table>

Urdu	Persian
آگ بن دهواں کہاں	هیچ دودی بی آتشی نیست
/ɒ:g bən dæhvan̲ kəhɒ:n̲/	/hi:tʃ du:di: bi: ɒ:tæʃi: ni:st/
Morovvat, 2007:2.	*Dehkhoda, 1984: 2016.*

Proverb's English equivalent: ***No smoke without fire***

The 13th century French phrase *"nul feu est sens fumee ne fumee sens feu"* (there is no fire without smoke [and] no smoke without fire) is the root of the proverb.

c **1375** J. BARBOUR *Bruce* (EETS) IV. **81** And thair may no man fire sa covir, [Bot] low or reyk1 sall it discovir2.]

c **1422** HOCCLEVE *Works* (EETS) I. **134** Wher no fyr maad is may no smoke aryse.

1592 G.DELAMOTHE *French Alphabet* II. **39** No smoke without fire.

1655 T. FULLER *Church Hist. Britain* II. x. There was no Smoak but some fire: either he was dishonest, or indiscreet.

1869 TROLLOPE *He knew He was Right* II. lii. He considered that … Emily Trevelyan had behaved badly. He constantly repeated … the old adage, that there was no smoke without fire

1948 M. INNES *Night of Errors* iv. 'Chimneys! … Who the deuce

---

[1] low or reyk, flame or smoke
[2] reveal

cares whether there's smoke from every chimney in the house.' 'I do. No smoke without fire.'

1976 D. STOREY *Saville* IV. xix. 'There's no smoke without fire.' 'And the way you're going about it you'll have it like a furnace when there's really nothing there at all.'

Urdu	Persian
آگ کہنے سے منہ نہیں جلتا	زبانم که نسوخت
/ɒːg kəhni: si: mənə nəhi:n̪ jəltɒ:/	/zæbɒːnæm kə næsuːχt/
Morovvat, 2007:2.	Dehkhoda, 1984: 894.
(معنای برابر فارسی= از گفتن آتش زبان نسوزد)	
Persian Equivalent Meaning:	
/æz goftænə ɒːtæʃ zæbɒːn	

Proverb's English equivalent: ***Hard words break no bones***

1697 G. MERITON *Yourkshire Ale* (ed. *3*) **84** Foul words break neay Banes.

1806 H. H. BRACKENRIDGE *Gazette Publications* **250** Hard words, and language break nae bane.

1814 G. MORRIS *Letter* **18** Oct. (**1889**) II. xlix. These ... are mere words- hard words, if you please, but they break no bones.

1882 BLACKMORE *Christowell* III. xvi. 'Scoundrel, after all that I have done__.' 'Hard words break no bones, my friend.'

1980 G. NELSON *Charity's Child* i. Soft words! They butter no parsnips ... Would you prefer hard ones? ... Hard words break no bones.

Proverb's English equivalent: ***Sticks and stones may break my bones, but words will never hurt me***

1894 G. F. NORTHALL *Folk–Phrases* **23** Sticks and stones will break my bones, but names will never hurt me! Said by one youngster to another calling names.

1980 *Cosmopolitan* Dec. **137** 'Sticks and stones may break my bones,' goes the children's rhyme, 'but words will never hurt me.' One wonders whether the people on the receiving end … would agree.

Urdu	Persian
آنکھوں پر پلکوں کا بوجھ نہیں ہوتا /ɒːnkhuːn̪ pər pəlkuːn̪ kɒː buːd͡ʒh nəhiːn̪ hotɒː/ *Morovvat, 2007:2.*	مژه به چشم زیادتی نکند /moʒə bə t͡ʃæʃm zjɒːdæːtiː næːkonæːd/ *Dehkhoda, 1984: 1707.*

Proverb's English equivalent: ***Blood is thicker than water***

The German phrase *"Ouch hoer ich sagen, daz sippebluot von wassere niht verdirbet"* is the root of the proverb. The oldest German usage goes back to the twelfth century, 1130 : 'Reinecke Fuch' (circa 1130 'Reynald the Fox'). But still some paremiologists believe the English resemble has its root in a Scottish phrase of the 19th century, and when the master of an American navy vessel, Captain Josiah Tattnall, proceeded to help an English navy vessel in Chinese river of Pei-ho in June *1859,* and he used the phrase *"blood is thicker than water"*, the proverb became common in English speaking societies.

1412 LYDGATE *Troy Book* (EETS) III. **2071** For naturely blod will ay of kynde Draw vn–to blod, wher he may it fynde.]

1813 J. RAY *English Proverbs* (ed. *5*) **281** Blood's thicker than water.

1815 SCOTT *Guy Mannering* II. xvii. Weel-blood's thicker than water– she's welcome to the cheeses.

1895 G. ALLEN *Woman who Did* xi. At moments of unexpected danger, angry feelings between father and son are often forgotten, and blood unexpectedly proves itself thicker than water.

1933 A. POWELL *From View to Death* iv. Really ... And then they say that blood is thicker than water. They know perfectly well that I have had hayfever.

1960 A. CHRISTIE *Adventures of Christmas Pudding* 240 It's exactly like a serial ... Reconciliation with the nephew, blood is thicker than water.

Urdu	Persian
اپنی چھاچھ کو کون کھٹا کہتا ہے /ɒːpəni: t͡ʃhæt͡ʃ ku: khu:n kəhtɒ: kəhtɒ: hə/ *Morovvat, 2007:2.*	کس نگوید که دوغ من ترش است /kæs nægu:jæd kə du:ɣ ə mæn torʃ æst/ *Dehkhoda, 1984: 1206.*

Proverb's English equivalent: ***Everyone speaks well of the bridge which carries him over***

1678 J. RAY *English Proverbs* (ed. 2) 106 Let every man praise the bridge he goes over. i. e. Speak not ill of him who hath done you a courtesie, or whom you have made use of to your benefit; or do commonly make use of.

1797 F. BAILY *Journal* 11 May (1856) 279 Let every one speak well of the bridge which carries him over. 1850 KINGSLEY Alton Locke I. x. Every one speak well of the bridge which carries him safe over. Every one fancies the laws which fill his pockets to be God's laws.

1886 G. DAWSON *Biographical Lectures* i. Our love of compromise … has also been our great strength … We speak well of the bridge that carries us over.

Urdu	Persian
اپنی گلی میں کتا بھی شیر ہوتا ہے	سگ در خانه صاحبش شیر است
/ɒːpəniː goliː məin kotɒː bəhiː ʃiːr hotɒː hə/	/sæg dær ə χɒːnəjə sɒːhəbæʃ ʃiːr æst/
Morovvat, 2007:2.	*Dehkhoda, 1984: 984.*

Proverb's English equivalent: ***Every cock will crow upon his own dunghill***

This proverb which is in use since the 1st century in Latin language, since the middle of the 13th century is used in English. The oldest form is the phrase "*gallum in suo sterquilinio plurimum posse*" which is used by Annaeus Lucius Seneca to lampoon Claudius, which had a French origin, in his book of *Apocolocyntosis,* nowadays known as book of *The Pumpkinification of Claudius.*

a **1250** *Ancrene Wisse* (**1952**) **62** Coc is kenel on his owune mixerne.2

1387 J. TREVISA tr. *Higden's Polychronicon* (**1879**) VIII. *5* As Seneca seith, a cok is most mighty on his dongehille.

1546 J. HEYWOOD *Dialogue of Proverbs* I. xi. D**2** He was at home there, he myght speake his will. Euery cocke is proude on his owne dunghill.

1771 SMOLLETT *Humphry Clinker* II. **178** Insolence... akin to the arrogance of the village cock, who never crows but upon his own dunghill.

---

[1] bold
[2] midden, dunghill

1935 D. L. SAYERS *Gaudy Night* xix. 'I believe you're showing off.' ... 'Every cock will crow upon his own dunghill.'

1980 M. GILBERT *Death of Favourite Girl* vii. Mariner seemed to be easy enough. A cock on his own dunghill.

Urdu	Persian
اپنے کیے کا علاج نہیں	خودکرده را تدبیر نیست
/ɒːpəni: kəi: kɒː əlɒːd͡ʒ nəhi:n̪/	/χodkærdə rɒː tædbi:r ni:st/
Morovvat. 2007:2.	*Dehkhoda, 1984: 755.*

Proverb's English equivalent: ***As you bake, so shall you brew***

c **1577** Misogonus III. i. As thou bakst, so shat brewe.

1775 D. GARRICK *May- Day* ii. To keep... My bones whole and tight, To speak, nor look, would I dare; As they bake they shall brew.

1909 W. DE MORGAN *It never can happen Again* I. v. Each one [i. e. young person]... was... the centre of an incubation of memories that were to last a lifetime. 'As they bake, so they will brew,' philosophized Mr. Challis to himself.

Proverb's English equivalent: ***As you brew, so shall you bake***

[**1264** in C. BROWN *English Lyrics of XIIIth Century* (**1932**) **131** Let him habbe ase he brew, bale to dryng.1 *a* **1325** Cursor Mundi (EETS) l. **2848** Nathing of that land vn–sonken,2 Suilk3 als thai brued now ha that dronken.

---

[1] literally, 'let him have as he brews, bale [i. e. evil, injury, misery] to drink'
[2] not sunken or submerged in water
[3] such

c **1450** *Towneley Play of Second Shepherd* (EETS) l. *501* Bot we must drynk as we brew And that is bot reson.]

c **1570** T. INGELEND *Disobedient Child* D8ᵛ As he had brewed, that so shulde bake.

1766 COLMAN & GARRICK *Clandestine Marriage* I. *3* As you sow, you must reap– as you brew, so you must bake.

1922 S. J. WEYMAN *Ovington's Bank* xxiii. No, you may go, my lad. As you ha' brewed you may bake.

Urdu	Persian
اچھے کو اچھا، برے کو برا کہتے ہیں	بد را باید بد گفت، خوب را خوب
/æt͡ʃhi: ku: æt͡ʃhɒ: bəri: ku: bərɒ: kəhti: həjn̪/	/bæd rɒ: bɒːjæd bæd goft χu:b rɒ: χu:b/
Morovvat, 2007:2.	*Dehkhoda, 1984: 402.*

Proverb's English equivalent: *To give the Devil his due*

1589 LYLY *Pap with Hatchet* III. 407 Giue them their due though they were diuels … and excuse them for taking anie money at interest.

1596 NASHE *Saffron Walden* III. 36 Giue the diuell his due.

[**1597–8** SHAKESPEARE Henry IV Pt. 1 He will give the Devil his due]

1642 *Prince Rupert's Declaration* 2 The Cavaliers (to give the Divell his due) fought very valiantly.

1751 SMOLLETT *Peregrine Pickle* I. xvii. You always used me in an officer–like manner, that I must own, to give the devil his due.

1936 H. AUSTIN *Murder of Matriarch* xxiii. To give the devil his due … I don't think that Irvin planned to incriminate anyone else.

1978 R. L. HILL *Evil that Men Do* vi. Giving the devil his due will always jostle the angels.

1998 WOOFENDEN *Satan, At Your Service* This is one way we must give the devil his due. For if greed and self-centeredness were not such great motivators, much less would be getting accomplished in our world--which has more than its share of greedy, selfish people. Still, if we look deeper, it is really not the devil accomplishing the good, but the Lord turning our greed and selfishness toward good purposes.

2000 CHARLES BRADLAUGH *Bank Of Wisdom* I am unable to say, certainly, whether I am writing about a singular Devil or a plurality of Devils. In one text "Devils" are mentioned (Lev 17:7), recognizing a plurality; in another, "the Devil," as if there was but one (Luke 4:2). We may, however, fairly assume that either there is one Devil, more than one, or less than one; and, having thus cleared our path from mere numerical difficulties we will proceed to give the Devil his due.

2004 SCHRIS KLITZING *Living The World* As I sit here and write this, I have to give the Devil his due. You look around and see all the split homes due to divorce.

<table>
<tr><th>Urdu</th><th>Persian</th></tr>
<tr><td>

احمد کی پگڑی محمود کے سر

/æhmæd ki: pægæri: mæhmu:d ki: sær/

Morovvat, 2007:2.

(معنای برابر فارسی= کلاہِ احمد سرِ محمود)

Persian Equivalent Meaning:

/kolæh ə æhmæd sær ə mæhmu:d/

</td><td>

کلاه احمد را سر محمود گذاشتن

/kolæh ə æhmæd rɒ: sær ə mæhmu:d gozɒ:ʃtæn/

Dehkhoda, 1984: 1224.

</td></tr>
</table>

Proverb's English equivalent: ***Robbing Peter to pay Paul***

1842 ASSOCIATION OF DEMOCRATS OF DUTCHESS COUNTY *The Anti-Bank Democrat (The Corporate Banking System)* We have all, probably, heard of that eccentric individual who was in the habit of settling his indebtedness to Paul by stealing the required amount from Peter; or in the words of the adage, "By robbing Peter to pay Paul."

2003 *Robbing Peter To Pay Paul* - "The expression 'rob Peter to pay Paul' goes back at least to John Wycliffe's 'Select English Works,' written in about **1380**. Equally old in French, the saying may derive from a 12th century Latin expression referring to the Apostles: 'As it were that one would crucify Paul in order to redeem Peter.' The words usually mean to take money for one thing and use it for another, especially in paying off debts," according to the "Encyclopedia of Word and

Phrase Origins" by ROBERT HENDRICKSON (*Fact on File*, New York, 1997) ".In 1546, it was included in John Heywood's collection of proverbs: 'To rob Peter to pay Paul.' George Herbert listed it in his collection (1640) as 'Give not Saint Peter so much, to leave Saint Paul nothing.' First attested in the United States in '*Thomas Hutchinson Papers*' (1657).

Urdu	Persian
ادھار محبت کی قینچی ہے	قرض مقراض محبت است
/ædhɒːr mohæbbæt kiː Giːntʃiː hə/	/Gærz məGrɒːzə mohæbbæt æst/
Morovvat, 2007:2.	دهخدا: قرض شوی مردانست
	/Gærz ʃuːjə mærdɒːn æst/
	Dehkhoda, 1984: 1159.

Proverb's English equivalent: ***Lend your money and lose your friend***

1999 HARIJS MARSAVS *English For Intermediate Students* … F. W. Shakespeare. All The World S A Stage … Jealous in honour, sudden and quick in quarrel, Seeking the bubble reputation Even in the cannon's mouth. And then the justice, In fair round belly with good capon lind, With eyes severe, and beard of formal cut, Full of wise saws and modern instances; And so he plays his part. The sixth age shifts Into the lean and slipper d pantaloon, With spectacles on nose and pouch on side; His youthful hose, well sav d, a world too wide For his shrunk shank; and his big manly voice Turning again toward childish treble, pipes And whistles in his sound. Last scene of all, That ends this strange history, Is second childishness, a mere oblivion, Sans teeth, sans eyes, sans taste, sans everything. *5*. Interpret the English proverbs and find their equivalents in Latvian. **1**. Before you make a friend eat a bushel of salt with him. **2**. The best of friends must part. **3**. Better an open enemy than a false friend. **4**. Better lose a jest than a friend. **5**. He that has a full purse never wanted a friend. **6**. A hedge between keeps the friendship green. **7**. Out of sight, out of mind. **8**. Among friends all things are common. **9**. Lend your money and lose your friend. **10**. Know your own faults before blaming others for theirs …

<table>
<tr><td align="center">Urdu</td><td align="center">Persian</td></tr>
<tr><td>

اشراف گھوڑے کو چابک کی حاجت نہیں

/æʃrɒːf ghuːriː kuː t͡ʃɒːbuːk kiː hɒːd͡ʒæt nəhiːn̪/

Morovvat, 2007:2.

</td><td>

اسب نجیب را یک تازیانه بس است

/æsbə næd͡ʒiːb rɒː jək tɒːzjɒːnə bæs æst/

Dehkhoda, 1984: 169.

</td></tr>
</table>

Proverb's English equivalent: ***A word to the wise is enough***

The Latin phrase of "*Verbum sat sapienti*" is the root of the proverb.

a **1513** DUNBAR *Poems* (**1979**) **206** Few wordis may serve the wyis.

1546 J. HEYWOOD *Dialogue of Proverbs* II. vii. I4v Fewe woords to the wise suffice to be spoken.

a **1605** W. HAUGHTON *Englishmen for My Money* (**1616**) D3 They say, a word to the Wise is enough: so by this little French that he speakes, I see he is the very man I seeke for.

1768 STERNE *Sentimental Journey* III. **164** A word, Mons. Yorick, to the wise... is enough.

1841 DICKENS *Old Curiosity Shop* ii. 'Fred!' cried Mr. Swiveller, tapping his nose, 'a word to the wise is sufficient for them – we may be good and happy without riches, Fred.'

a **1947** F. THOMPSON *Still Glides Stream* (**1948**) vi. I advise you to keep an eye on that eldest daughter of yours... You know what they say, a word to the wise.

1968 M. WOODHOUSE *Rock Baby* xi. Some undesirable elements around. Word to the wise, eh?

<table>
<tr><td align="center">Urdu</td><td align="center">Persian</td></tr>
<tr><td align="center">اللـہ کی لاٹھی میں آواز نہیں</td><td align="center">چوب خدا صدا ندارد</td></tr>
<tr><td>/ællɒ:h ki: lɒ:thi: məjn ɒ:vɒ:z nəhi:n̪/

Morovvat, 2007:2.</td><td>/t͡ʃu:b ə χodɒ: sədɒ: næd ɒ:ræd/

Dehkhoda, 1984: 632.</td></tr>
</table>

Proverb's English equivalent: ***The mills of God grind slowly, yet they grind exceeding small***

The Greek phrase of "*ὀψέ θεῶν ἀλέουσι μύλοι, ἀλέουσι δέ λεπτά*" is the root of the proverb, Sextus *Empiricus Against Professors* I. 287.

1640 G. HERBERT *Outlandish Proverbs* no. **747** Gods Mill grinds slow, but sure.

1870 LONGFELLOW *Poems* (**1960**) **331** Though the mills of God grind slowly, yet they grind exceeding small; Though with patience he stands waiting, with exactness grind he all.

1942 F. BEEDING *Twelve Disguises* i. That's my business ... The mills of God grind slowly, but they grind exceeding small.

1979 G. SWARTOUT *Skeletons* **81** The law should have been allowed to take its course. The mills of the gods grind slowly, it is true, but in time, in time - .

<table>
<tr><td align="center">Urdu</td><td align="center">Persian</td></tr>
</table>

اندھوں میں کانا راجا	در شهر کوران، مرد یک چشم پادشاه است
/ændhu:n məjn kɒ:nɒ: rɒ:d͡ʒɒ:/	
Morovvat, 2007:3.	/dær ʃæhr ə ku:rɒ:n mærd ə jək t͡ʃəʃm pɒ:dəʃɒ:h æst/

Proverb's English equivalent: ***In the country of the blind, the one–eyed man is king***

The Latin phrase of "*In regione caecorum rex est luscus*" is the root of the proverb; ERASMUS *Adages* III. iv.

1522-23 SKELTON *Works* (**1843**) II. **43** An one eyed man is Well syghted when He is amonge blynde men.

1640 G. HERBERT *Outlandish Proverbs* no. **469** In the kingdome of blind men the one ey'd is king.

1830 J. L. BURCKHARDT *Arabic Proverbs* **34** The one–eyed person is a beauty in the country of the blind.

1904 H. G. WELLS in Strand Apr. **405** Through his thoughts ran this old proverb... 'In the Country of the Blind, the One–Eyed Man is king.'

1937 W. H. SAUMAREZ SMITH *Letter* **7** Mar. in *Young Man's Country* (**1977**) ii. You exaggerate the alleged compliment paid to me by the Bengal Govt. in wanting to retain my services. 'In the country of the blind the one–eyed man is king'.

1979 *Guardian* **3** Oct. **11** At last among the blind the one–eyed man was king... There are men much more limited than David.

Urdu	Persian
اندھے کودن رات برابر	مشابه:
/ændhi: ku:dən rɒ:t bærɒ:bər/ *Morovvat, 2007:3.*	چه برای کر بزنی، چه برای کور برقصی
(معنای برابر فارسی= برای کور شب و روز یکی است)	
Persian Equivalent Meaning:	Equivalent:
/bærɒ:j ə ku:r ʃæb o ru:z jəki: æst/	/t͡ʃə bærɒ:j ə ku:r bəzæni: t͡ʃə bəræGsi:/ *Dehkhoda, 1984: 673.*

Proverb's English equivalent: *A nod's as good as a wink to a blind horse*

1794 W. GODWIN *Caleb Williams* I. viii. Say the word; a nod is as good as a wink to a blind horse.

1822 B. MALKIN *Gil Blas* (rev. ed.) I. II. ix. I shall say no more at present; a nod is as good as a wink.

1879 R. M. BALLANTYNE *Six Months at the Cape* What tremendous floods are implied in the carrying away of this bridge! What superabundance of water in that so-called land of drought! What opportunities for engineering skill to catch and conserve the water, and turn the "barren land" into fruitful fields! Don't you see this, Periwinkle? If not, I will say no more, for, according to the proverb, "a nod is as good as a wink to the blind horse."

1925 S. O'CASEY *Shadow of Gunman in Two Plays* I. **142** You needn't say no more – a nod's as good as a wink to a blind horse.

1979 L. MEYNELL *Hooky & Villainous Chauffeur* vi. The way he behaves … Other men's wives. Still, I expect you know as much about that as I do … They say a nod's as good as a wink to a bilnd horse.

Proverb's English equivalent: *A nod is as good as a wink*

1822 SIR WALTER SCOTT *The Fortunes of Nigel Chapter* XXV. "Absurd!—Why, think you she will not have thee? Take her with the tear in her eye, man—take her with the tear in her eye. Let me hear from you to-morrow. Good-night, good-night—a nod is as good as a wink. I must to my business of sealing and locking up. By the way, this horrid work has put all out of my head.—Here is a fellow from Mr. Lowestoffe has been asking to see you. As he said his business was express, the Senate only made him drink a couple of flagons, and he was just coming to beat up your quarters when this breeze blew up.— Ahey, friend! there is Master Nigel Grahame."

Urdu	Persian
اونٹ چڑھے کتا کاٹے /uːnt t͡ʃærhiː kətɒː kɒːthiː/ *Morovvat, 2007:3.* (معنای برابر فارسی= بختِ بد سگ گَزَد) Persian Equivalent Meaning: /bæχt ə bæd sæg gæzæd/	بخت چون برگشت پالوده دندان بشکند /bæχt t͡ʃon bærgæʃt pɒːluːdəh dændɒːn bəʃkænæd/ *Dehkhoda, 1984: 393.*

Proverb's English equivalent: ***The bread never falls but on its buttered side***

1546 J. HEYWOOD *Dialogue of Proverbs* "I knowe on whiche syde my breade is buttred."

1564 *The Bullein Dialogue* "He knoweth vpon whiche side his breade is buttered well enough, I warrante you."

1867 A. D. RICHARDSON *Beyond Mississippi* iii. His bread never fell on the buttered side.

1891 J. L. KIPLING *Beast & Man* x. We express the completeness of ill–luck by saying, 'The bread never falls but on its buttered side.'

1906 JOHN GALSWORTHY *The Man of Property* "Bosinney looked clever, but he had also ... and it was one of his great attractions ... an air as if he did not quite know on which side his bread were buttered."

1929 A. GRAY *Dead Nigger* xix. Didn't her bread and butter always fall butter downwards?

1980 *Guardian* 3 Dec. 12 Murphy's (or Sod's) Law ... Murphy's many relatives always quote it as 'Buttered bread falls buttered side down – and if it's a sandwich it falls open.'

Proverb's English equivalent: *If anything can go wrong, it will*

1955 *Aviation Mechanics Bulletin* May–June 11 Murphy's Law: If an aircraft part can be installed incorrectly, someone will install it that way.

1956 *Scientific American* Apr. 166 Dr. Schaefer's observation confirms this department's sad experience that editors as well as laboratory workers are subject to Murphy's Laws, to wit: 1. If something can go wrong it will, [etc.].

1958 *Product Engineering* 21 Apr. 32 If anything can go wrong with an experiment–it will.

1961 LEEDS & WEINBERG *Computer Programming Fundamentals* viii. What we desire is the presentation of the information in ... an accurate and complete form ... Recalling 'Murphy's law' – 'If something can go wrong or be misinterpreted, it will' – should be enough stimulus for the goals we desire.

1974 *New York Times Magazine* 8 Sept. 33 'If anything can go wrong, it will,' says Murphy's law. In this computer age, the 'law' has been helped along by clever con men.

1980 A. E. FISHER *Midnight Men* vii. Of course, the up train was delayed. There was some vast universal principle. If anything can go wrong it will.

Urdu	Persian

ایک میان میں دو تلوار نہیں رہ سکتی

/əjk məjɒːn məjn do təlvɒːr nəhiːn̪ rəh sækt:/

Morovvat, 2007:3.

(معنای برابر فارسی= دو شمشیر در نیامی نگنجند)

Persian Equivalent Meaning:

/do ʃæmʃiːr dær nəjɒːmiː næɡoniæd/

دو پادشاه در اقلیمی نگنجند

/do pɒːdəʃɒːh dær əGliːmiː næɡonjænd/

Dehkhoda, 1984: 831.

Proverb's English equivalent: *If two ride on a horse, one must ride behind*

1598–9 SHAKESPEARE *Much Ado about Nothing* III. v. **34** An two men ride of a horse, one must ride behind.

c **1628** J. SMYTH *Berkeley MSS* (**1885**) III. **32** If two ride upon an horse one must sit behinde; meaninge, That in each contention one must take the foile1.

1874 G. J. WHYTE–MELVILLE *Uncle John* I. x. There is an old adage … 'When two people ride on a horse, one must ride behind.'

1942 V. RATH *Posted for Murder* VI. iii. There comes a point when you are very exasperating … 'When two ride on one horse, one must ride behind.' But I'm getting off for a while.

---

[1] repulse or defeat

<table>
<tr><td align="center">Urdu</td><td align="center">Persian</td></tr>
<tr><td align="center">

ایک ہاتھ سے تالی نہیں بجتی

/əjk hɒːtə siː tɒːliː nəhiːn bəd͡ʒətiː/

Morovvat, 2007:3.

</td><td align="center">

یک دست صدا ندارد

/jək dæst sədɒː næddɒːræd/

Dehkhoda, 1984: 2042.

</td></tr>
</table>

Proverb's English equivalent: ***It takes two to make a quarrel***

1706 J. STEVENS *Spanish & English Dict.* S. V. Barajar, When one will not, two do not Quarrel.

1732 T. FULLER *Gnomologia* no. **4942** There must be two at least to a Quarrel.

1859 H. KINGSLEY *Geoffrey Hamlyn* II. xiii. It takes two to make a quarrel, Cecil, and I will not be one.

1979 Times **3** Dec **13** If it were not for the truism that it takes at least two to make a quarrel, the French and the Germens … could fairly claim that the fault lay wholly with the United Kingdom.

Proverb's English equivalent: ***It takes two to tango***

1952 HOFFMAN & MANNING *Takes Two to Tango* (song title) **2** There are lots of things you can do alone! But, takes two to tango.

1965 *Listener* **24** June **923** As for negotiation … the President has a firm, and melancholy, conviction: it takes two to tango.

1974 G. JENKINS *Bridge of Magpies* vii. 'We're not getting anywhere.' 'It takes two to tango,' I said. 'I'll listen.'

1979 *Guardian* 4 Apr. **12** It takes two to tango … Mrs Thatcher has turned Mr Callaghan down.

Proverb's English equivalent: ***It takes two to make a bargain***

1598 Mucedorus B2 Nay, Soft, sir, tow words to a bargaine.

a **1637** MIDDLETON et al. *Widow* v. i. There's two words to a bargain ever … and if love be one, I'm sure money's the other.

1766 GOLDSMITH *Vicar of Wakefield* II. xii. 'Hold, hold, Sir,' cried Jenkinson, 'there are two words to that bargain.'

1943 M. FLAVIN *Journey in Dark* iv. Takes two to make a bargain, and you both done mighty wrong.

Proverb's English equivalent: ***Many hands make light work***

The proverb has its root in the Greek phrase of "πλείων μέν πλεόνων μελέτη" and the Latin phrase of "*Multae manus onus levius reddunt*"; Hesiod *Works & Days* **380**, Erasmus *Adages* II. iii. **95**.

c **1330** *Sir Beves* (EETS) l. **3352** Ascopard be strong & sterk,1 Mani hondes maketh light werk!

1678 BUTLER *Hudibras* III. ii. Most Hands dispatch apace, And make light work, (the proverb says).

---

[1] physically powerful

1721 J. KELLY *Scottish Proverbs* **244** Many Hands make light Work. Because it is but little to every one. **1923** Observer **11** Feb. **9** What is the use of saying that 'Many hands make light work' when the same copy–book tells you that 'Too many cooks spoil the broth'?

1978 L. EGAN *Dream Apart* ix. Well, Lorenzo … , you back again? Got the family with you this time, hah? Many hands make light work.

Urdu	Persian
بنیے کا سلام بے غرض نہیں ہوتا	سلام روستایی بی طمع نیست
/bəni: kɒ: sælɒːm biː ɣæræz nəhiːṉ hotɒː/	/sælɒːm ə ruːstɒːiː biː tæmæʔ niːst/
Morovvat, 2007: 3.	Dehkhoda, 1984: 989.

Proverb's English equivalent: ***Fear the Greeks bearing gifts***

The Italian phrase of "*Timeo Danaos, et dona ferentes*" is the root of the proverb.

1777 S. JOHNSON *Letter* 3 May (*1952*) II. *515* Tell Mrs. Boswell that I shall taste her marmalade cautiously at first. Timeo Danaos et dona ferentes. Beware, says the Italian proverb, of a reconciled enemy.]

1873 A. TROLLOPE *Phineas Redux* I. xxxiii. The right honourable gentleman had prided himself on his generosity as a Greek. He would remind the right honourable gentleman that presents from Greeks had ever been considered dangerous.

1929 *Times* 26 Oct. 13 Mr. Moses... must now be reflecting on the wisdom of the advice to 'fear the Greeks even when they bring gifts'.

1943 E. S. GARDNER *Case of Drowsy Mosquito* vi. ' It wasn't a trap, I tell you.' Nell Sims said ... 'Fear the Greeks when they bear olive branches.'

1980 J. GERSON *Assassination Run* iv. Fear the Greeks bearing gifts was the maxim to be drummed into every novice in ...

Urdu	Persian
بن روئے ماں بھی دودھ نہیں دیتی /bən ruːiː mɒːn bəhiː duːdu nəhiːṉ dəjtiː/ *Morovvat, 2007:3.* (معنای برابر فارسی= تا نگرید طفل کی نوشد لبن) Persian Equivalent Meaning: /tɒː nægərjæd təfl kəj nuːʃæd/ læbæn/	مشابه: تا نگرید ابر کی خندد چمن Equivalent: /tɒː nægərjæd æbr kəj χændæd t͡ʃæmæn/ *Dehkhoda, 1984:540.*

Proverb's English equivalent: *It is not spring until you can plant your foot upon twelve daisies*

1863 R. CHAMBERS Book of Days I. **312** We can now plant our 'foot upon nine daisies' and not until that can be done do the old-fashioned country people believe that spring is really come.

1878 T. F. THISELTON–DYER *English Folk–Lore* i. 'It ain't spring until you can plant your foot upon twelve daisies,' is a proverb still very prevalent.

1910 *Spectator* **26** Man **499** Spring is here when you can tread on nine daisies at once on the village green; so goes one of the country proverbs.

1972 CASSON & GRENFELL *Nanny Says* **52** When you can step on six daisies at once, summer has come.

Proverb's English equivalent: ***A dripping June sets all in tune***

1742 *Agreeable Companion* *35* A dripping June Brings all Things in Tune.

1883 W. ROPER *Weather Sayings* *22* A dry May and a dripping June brings all things in tune.

1912 *Spectator* *28* Dec. *1094* 'A dripping June sets all in tune,' and on sandy soils not only farm crops but garden flowers do best in a wet summer.

Urdu	Persian

بندے کا چاہاکچھ نہیں ہوتا ۔ اللہ کا چاہا سب کچھ ہوتا ہے

/bændi: kɒ: t͡ʃæhɒːkt͡ʃə nəhiːn̪ hotɒ:/ - /ællɒːh kɒ: t͡ʃəhɒː səb kət͡ʃə hotɒ: hə/

Morovvat, 2007:3.

هرچه دلم خواست نه آن می‌شود ۔ هرچه خدا خواست همان می‌شود

/hær t͡ʃə dəlæm χɒːst næh ɒːn mi: ʃævæd/ - /hær t͡ʃə χodɒː χɒːst hæmɒːn mi: ʃævæd/

Dehkhoda, 1984: 1921.

Proverb's English equivalent: ***Man proposes, God disposes***

The Latin phrase of "*Homo proponit, sed Deus disponit*" is the root of the proverb; T. à Kempis *De Imitatione Christi* I.xix.

c **1440** LYDGATE *Fall of Princes* (EETS) I. **3291** A man off malice may a thyng purpose ... But God a–boue can graciousli dispose1 Ageyn such malice to make resistence.

c **1450** tr. *T. à Kempis' De Imitatione Christi* (EETS) I. xix. For man purposith & god disposith.

1640 G. HERBERT *Outlandish Proverbs* no. **1** Man Proposeth, God disposeth.

1853 R. C. TRENCH *On Lessons in Proverbs* (ed. **2**) iii. A proverb ... Man proposes, God disposes ... that every nation in Europe possesses.

1958 L. DURRELL *Mountolive* IV. **88** In diplomacy one can only propose, never dispose. That is up to God, don't you think?

---

[1] determine or control the course of affairs or events

Urdu	Persian

بولنا چاندی ہے مگر خاموش رہنا سونا ہے

/buːlnɒː t͡ʃɒːndiː hə mægær ræhnɒː suːnɒː hə/

Morovvat, 2007:3.

اگر گفتن سیم است، خاموشی زر است

/ægær goftæn siːm æst χɒːmuːʃiː zær æst/

Dehkhoda, 1984: 226.

Proverb's English equivalent: ***Silence is golden***

1865 W. WHITE *Eastern England* II. ix. Silence is golden, says the proverb. We apprehend the full significance... in some lone hamlet situate amid a 'thousand fields'.

1923 A. HUXLEY *Antic Hay* xx. Silence is golden, as her father used to say when she used to fly into tempers and wanted to say nasty things to everybody within range.

1980 J. O'NEILL *Spy Game* xxv. 'I'll tell you the rest … on the way back.' He sealed her lips with a finger.' Meanwhile, silence is golden.'

Proverb's English equivalent: ***Speech is silver, but silence is golden***

1834 CARLYLE in FRASER's June *668* As the Swiss Inscription says: Sprechen ist silbern, Schweigen ist golden (Speech is silvern, Silence is golden).

1865 A. RICHARDSON *Secret Service* ii. A taciturn but edified listener, I pondered upon … 'speech is silver, while silence is golden'.

1936 W. HOLTBY *South Riding* I. iv. She will give a pound note to the collection if I would cut my eloquence short, so in this case, though speech is silver, silence is certainly golden.

1961 M. SPARK *Prime of Miss Jean Brodie* i. Speech is silver but silence is golden. Mary, are you listening?

Urdu	Persian
بہشت ماں کے قدموں تکے ہے	بهشت زیر پای مادران باشد
/bəhəʃt mɒ:n ki: Gædæmu:n təki: hə/	/bəhəʃt zi:r ə pɒ:j ə mɒ:dærɒ:n æst/
Morovvat, 2007:3.	Dehkhoda, 1984: 480.

Proverb's English equivalent: ***The hand that rocks the cradle rules the world***

1865 W. R. WALLACE in J. K. HOYT *Cyclopædia of Practical Quotations* (1896) 402 A mightier power and stronger Man from his throne has hurled, For the hand that rocks the cradle Is the hand that rules the world.

a **1916** SAKI *Toys of Peace* (1919) 158 You can't prevent it; it's the nature of the sex. The hand that rocks the cradle rocks the world, in a volcanic sense.

1979 *Guardian* 12 June 9 The hand that rocks the cradle may rule the world but... the hand itself is controlled by the state.

Urdu	Persian
بے‌کاری سے بیگاری بھلی	بیگاری به که بیکاری
/biːkɒːriː siː biːgɒːriː bəhliː/	/biːgɒːriː bəh kə biːkɒːriː/
Morovvat, 2007:3.	*Dehkhoda, 1984: 490.*

Proverb's English equivalent: ***Better wear out than to rust out***

[**1557** R. EDGEWORTH *Sermons* A1ᵛ Better it is to shine with laboure, then to rouste for idlenes.]

1598 SHAKESPEARE *Henry* IV, Pt. 2 I. ii. 206, I were better to be eaten to death with a rust than to be scoured to nothing with perpetual motion.[1]

1820 in Southey *Life of Wesley* II. xxv. I had rather wear out than rust out.

1834 M. EDGEWORTH *Helen* II. xiii. Helen... trembled for her health... but she repeated her favourite maxim – 'Better to wear out, than to rust out.'

1947 S. BELLOW *Victim* xvii. It was better to wear out than to rust out, as was often quoted. He was a hard worker himself.

1972 *Times* 24 May 16 'A man will rust out sooner'n he'll wear out' is one of his oft-repeated maxims.

---

[1] the sense is inverted in this quotation

Urdu	Persian
پوچھتے پوچھتے خدا کا گھر مل جاتا ہے	پرسان پرسان می‌روند (به) هندوستان
/puːt͡ʃhtiː puːt͡ʃhtiː χuːdɒː kɒː Gæhær məl d͡ʒɒːtɒː hə/	/porsɒːn porsɒːn miːrævænd (bə) hənduːstɒːn/
Morovvat, 2007:3.	*Dehkhoda, 1984: 502.*
(معنای برابر فارسی= پرسان پرسان به کعبه می‌توان رفت)	
Persian Equivalent Meaning:	
/porsɒːn porsɒːn bə kæəbə miː tævɒːn ræft/	

Proverb's English equivalent: *He that nothing questioneth nothing (will) learneth*

(1608 -1661) THOMAS FULLER *Great Christian Quotes* He that nothing questioneth, nothing learneth ... J. E. TWEED, M. A., CHAPLAIN OF CHRIST CHURCH Expositions On The Book Of Psalms *Abridged from the six volumes of the Oxford Psalms* 119-124: From The 5th Book Of The Psalms Psalm CXIX. (2) He questioneth himself, and answereth himself. Wherewithal?" So far it is a question: next cometh the answer, "even by keeping Thy words." But in this place the keeping of the words of God, must be understood as the obeying His commandments in deed: for they are kept in memory in vain, if they are not kept in life also. But what is meant by "young man" here?

Urdu	Persian
جب خدا دینے پر آتا ہے تو پھر یہ نہیں کہتا کہ تو کون ہے	مشابہ:

/d͡ʒəb χu:dɒ: dəjni: pær ɒ:tɒ: hə tu:phərjə nəhi:n̪ kəhtɒ: kə tu: kon hə/

Morovvat, 2007:3.

(معنای برابر فارسی= خدا وقتی می‌دهد نمی‌پرسد کیستی)

Persian Equivalent Meaning:

/χodɒ: væGti: mi: dæhæd nəmi: porsæd ki:sti:/

هر کسی خدایی دارد ـ قسمتی جدایی دارد

Equivalent:

/hær kæsi: χodɒ:i: dɒ:ræd – Gəsmæti: jodɒ:i: dɒ:ræd/

Dehkhoda, 1984: 1942.

Proverb's English equivalent: *Every elm has its man*

[**1906** KIPLING *Puck of Pook's Hill* **32** Ellum she hateth mankind, and waiteth Till every gust be laid To drop a limb on the head of him That any way trusts her shade.]

1928 *Times* **29** Nov. **10** Owing to the frequency with which this tree sheds its branches, or is uprooted in a storm, it has earned for itself a sinister reputation. 'Every elm has its man' is an old country saying.

<table>
<tr><th>Urdu</th><th>Persian</th></tr>
<tr><td>

جس کا کوئی نہیں اس کا خدا

ʤəs kɒː koi: nəhi:n̪ əs kɒː/
/ χuːdɒː

Morovvat, 2007:3.

</td><td>

خدا کس بی کسان است

/χodɒː kæs ə biːkæsɒːn æst/

</td></tr>
</table>

Proverb's English equivalent: ***Man's extremity is God's opportunity***

1629 T. ADAMS *Works* **619** Heere is now a deliuery fit for God, a cure for the Almightie hand to vndertake. Mans extremity is Gods opportunitie.

1706 LD. BELHAVEN in Defoe *Hist. Union* (**1709**) v. **34** Man's Extremity is God's opportunity ... ome unforeseen Providence will fall out, that may cast the Balance.

1916 E. A. BURROUGHS *Valley of* Decision viii. In the first winter of the war ... we were all much encouraged by tales of a new thirst for religion among the majority of the men... 'Man's extremity, God's opportunity.'

1949 D. SMITH *I capture Castle* xiii. '... the church if ever you're mantally run down.' ... 'You mean "Man's extremity is God's opportunity"? '

1980 *Times* **4** Dec. **17** Those extremities which have, until now, been often God's opportunity.

<table>
<tr><th>Urdu</th><th>Persian</th></tr>
<tr><td>

جلدی کا کام شیطان کا

/d͡ʒældi: kɒ: kæm ʃəjtɒ:n kɒ:/

Morovvat, 2007:3.

</td><td>

عجله کار شیطان است

/æd͡ʒælə kɒ:r ə ʃəjtɒ:n æst/

Dehkhoda, 1984: 1090.

</td></tr>
</table>

Proverb's English equivalent: ***Make haste slowly***

The Latin phrase of *"festina lente"* is the root of the proverb.

[L *festina lente* make haste slowly; after SUETONIUS *Augustus* xxv. **4** *nihil autem mins perfecto duci quam festinationem temeritatemque convenire arbitratur. Crebro itaque illa iactabat:* σπεῦδεβοαδέως, he [Augstus] thought that delay and reshness were alike unsuited to a well–trained leader. So he often came out with sayings like 'make haste slowly' [etc.]; cf. *c* **1385** CHAUCER *Troilus & Criseyde* I. **956** He hasteth wel tha wisly kan[1] abyde.]

1683 DRYDEN *Poems* (**1958**) I. **336** Gently make hase ... A hundred times consider what you've said.

1744 B. FRANKLIN *Poor Richard' Almanack* (Apr.) Make haste slowly.

1938 M. TEAGLE *Murders in Silk* iii. Easy, son. Let's make haste slowly. Does Conner know where the knife came from?

---

[1] knows how to

Proverb's English equivalent: ***More haste, less speed***

c **1350** Douce MS *52* no. **86** The more hast, the worse spede.

1549 J. HEYWOOD Dialogue of Proverbs I. ii. A3ᵛ Moste tymes he seeth, the more haste the lesse speede.

1595 *Locrine* (**1908**) I. ii. My penne is naught; gentlemen, lend me a knife. I thinke the more haste the worst speed.

1705 E. WARD *Hudibras Redivivus* I. i. A mod'rate pace is best indeed. The greater hurry, the worse speed.

1887 BLACKMORE *Springhaven* III. xi. Some days had been spent by the leisurely Dutchman in providing fresh supplies, and the stout bark's favourite maxim seemed to be- 'the more haste the less speed.'

1919 S. J. WEYMAN *Great House* xxvii. Tell me the story from the beginning. And take time. More haste, less speed, you know.

1979 P. NIESEWAND *Member of Club* xvi. If they'd taken a bit more time with the terrorist he'd have told them everything... More haste, less speed.

Proverb's English equivalent: ***Nothing should be done in haste but gripping a flea***

a **1655** N. L' ESTRANGE in *Anecdotes & Traditions* (**1839**) I. *55* A grave gentleman in this Kingdome us'd this phrase often: 'Do nothing rashly, but catching of fleas.'

1678 J. RAY *English Proverbs* (ed. **2**) **151** Nothing most be done hastily but killing of fleas.

1721 J. KELLY *Scottish Proverbs* **261** Nothing to be done in haste, but gripping of Fleas ... Spoken when we are unreasonably urged to make haste.

1927 J. BUCHAN *Witch Wood* xii. What's the need o' hurry when the body's leg is still to set. As my auld mither used to say, naething suld be done in haste but grippin' a flea. [Cf. **1981** Daily Telegraph **16** July **18** Mr.Whitelaw ... has not taken shelter behind the often disastrously misleading maxim that' nothing should be done in hot blood'.]

Urdu	Persian
جہاں گل ہوگا، وہاں خار بھی ضرور ہوگا	مشابه:
/dʒæhɒːn guːl hogɒː væhɒːn χɒːr bəhiː zæruːr hogɒː/	هر جا که پریرخی است دیوی با اوست
Morovvat, 2007:3.	
(معنای برابر فارسی= هر جا گلی است خاری در پهلوی اوست)	/hær dʒɒː kə pæriː roχiː æst diːviː bɒː uːst/
Persian Equivalent Meaning:	*Dehkhoda, 1984: 1912.*
/hær dʒɒː goliː æst χɒːriː dær pæhluːjə uːst/	

Proverb's English equivalent: ***Where God builds a church, the Devil*** will build a chapel

1590 T. BECON *Works* I. *516*ᵛ For commonly, where so ever God buildeth a church, the Deuyll wyl builde a Chappell iuste by.

1701 DEFOE *True-born Englishman* 4 Wherever God erects a House of Prayer, The Devil always builds a Chapel there: And 'twill be found upon Examination, The latter has the largest Congregation.

1903 G. H. KNIGHT *Master's Questions* xiii. Nowhere does the devil build his little chapels more cunningly than close under the shadow of the great temple of Christian liberty. A thing in itself completely right and good, may be, in its effects on others, completely evil.

Urdu	Persian

جہاں گنج، وہاں رنج

/dʒæhɒ:n gænd͡ʒ væhɒ:n rænd͡ʒ /

Morovvat, 2007:3.

مشابه:

نابرده رنج گنج میسر نمی‌شود

Equivalent:

/nɒ:bordə rænd͡ʒ gænd͡ʒ mojæssær nəmi: ʃævæd/

Dehkhoda, 1984: 1780.

Proverb's English equivalent: ***Nothing venture, nothing gain***

c **1385** CHAUCER *Troilus & Criseyde* II. **807** He which that nothing under-taketh, Nothyng n'acheveth, be hym looth or deere1.

1481 CAXTON *Reynard* (**1880**) xii. [He that will wynne he muste laboure and auenture.]

1546 J. HEYWOOD *Dialogue of Proverbs* I.xi.E1 Noght venter noght haue.

1559 T. COOPER *Bibliotheca Proverbs* (ed. **3**) s.v. Fortis, Fortune foretherethe2 bolde aduenturers, nothyng venture, nothyng haue.

1624 T. HEYWOOD *Captives* IV. i. I see hee that nought venters,

---

[1] be hym looth or deere, whether hateful or pleasing to him
[2] i.e. furthers

nothinge gaynes.

1668 C. SEDLEY *Mulberry Garden* III. ii. Who ever caught any thing With a naked hook? nothing venture, nothing Win.

1791 BOSWELL *Life of Johnson* II. **166**, I am, however, generally for trying 'Nothing venture, nothing have.'

1841 CHARLES DICKENS *Old Curiosity Shop* I. xxix. I'm sorry the gentlemen's daunted -- nothing venture, nothing have -- but the gentleman knows best.

1876 BLACKMORE *Cripps* III. iv. We must all have been in France ... if -- well, never mind. Nothing venture, nothing win.

1937 A. CHRISTIE *Death on Nile* II. xxix. Nothing venture nothing have! It's about the only time in my life I shall be near to touching a fat lot of money.

1967 D. MORRIS *Naked Ape* iv. For him [the withdrawn individual] the old saying:'Nothing ventured, nothing gained' has been re-written: 'Nothing ventured, nothing lost'.

1979 A. PRICE *Tomorrow's Ghost* vii. That was decidedly interesting -- 'And Pearson Cole?' Nothing venture, nothing gain.

Proverb's English equivalent: ***Put a stout heart to a stay brae***

a **1585** A. MONTGOMERIE *Cherry & Sloe* (**1821**) xxxvi. So gets ay, that sets ay, Stout stomackis to the brae[1].

---

[1] slope or hill–side

1721 J. KELLY *Scottish Proverbs* **287** Set a stout Heart to a stay[1] Brea. Set about a difficult Business with Courage and Constancy.

1821 J. GALT *Annals of Parish* i. I began a round of visitations; but oh, it was a steep brae that I had to climb, and it needed a stout heart. For I found the doors … barred against me.

1916 J. BUCHAN *Greenmantle* xii. He … shouted to me … to 'pit a stoot hert tae a stey brae'.

Proverb's English equivalent: *Nothing venture, nothing have*

1651 FANSHAWE *Memoirs of Lady Ann Fanshawe* At last came the captain and a soldier with your father, who was very cheerful in appearance; who, after he had spoke and saluted me and his friends there, said, 'Pray let us not lose time, for I know not how little I have to spare. This is the chance of war - Nothing venture, nothing have; and so let us sit down and be merry whilst we may.' Then taking my hand in his, and kissing me, said, 'Cease weeping; no other thing upon earth can move me. Remember we are all at God's dispose.'

1840-41 CHARLES DICKENS *The Old Curiosity Shop* Look at them. See what they are and what thou art. Who doubts that we must win!' 'The gentleman has thought better of it, and isn't coming,' said Isaac, making as though he would rise from the table. 'I'm sorry the gentleman's daunted--nothing venture, nothing have--but the gentleman knows best.' 'Why I am ready. You have all been slow but me,' said the old man. 'I wonder who is more anxious to begin than I.'

----

[1] steep

<table>
<tr><th>Urdu</th><th>Persian</th></tr>
<tr><td>

ضرورت ایجاد کی ماں ہے

/zəru:ræt i:d͡ʒɒ:d ki: mɒ:n hə/

Morovvat, 2007:3.

</td><td>

احتیاج مادر اختراع است

/əhtjɒ:d͡ʒ mɒ:dær ə əχtərɒ:ʔ æst/

Dehkhoda, 1984: 88.

</td></tr>
</table>

Proverb's English equivalent: ***Necessity is the mother of invention***

[**1519** W. HORMAN *Vulgaria* **52** Nede taught hym wytte. Necessitas ingenium dedit.]

1545 R. ASCHAM *Toxophilus* II. **18**ᵛ Necessitie, the inuentor of all good–nesse (as all authours in a maner, doo saye) ... inuented a shaft heed.

1608 G. CHAPMAN *Tragedy of Byron* IV. i. The great Mother, Of all productions (graue Necessity).

1658 R. FRANCK *Northern Memoirs* (**1694**) 44 Art imitates Nature, and Necessity is the Mother of Invention.

1726 SWIFT *Gulliver's Travels* IV. X. I soaled my Shoes with wood, which I cut from a Tree ... No man could more verify the Truth ... That, Necessity is the Mother of Invention.

1861 C. READE *Cloister & Hearth* II. vi. 'But, dame, I found language too poor to paint him. I was fain to invent. You know Necessity is the mother of - .' 'Ay! ay, that is old enough, o' conscience.'

1974 A. PRICE *Other Paths to Glory* I. vi. Necessity has been once more the mother of invention. I have invented Captain Lefevre.

Urdu	Persian
عقلمند کو ایک اشاره کافی ہے	آن کس است اهل بشارت که اشارت داند
/æGlmænd ko i:k əʃɒ:ræ kɒ:fi: hə/	/ɒ:n kæs æst æhl ə bəʃɒ:ræt kə əʃɒ:ræt dɒ:næd/
Morovvat, 2007:3.	*Dehkhoda. 1984: 59.*

Proverb's English equivalent: ***A word to the wise***

The Latin phrase of "*Verbum sat sapienti*" is the root of the proverb.

1758 BENJAMIN FRANKLIN *The Way to Wealth* I have heard, that nothing gives an author so great pleasure as to find his works respectfully quoted by others. Judge, then, how much I must have been gratified by an incident I am going to relate, to you. Istopped my horse lately, where a great number of people were collected at an auction of merchants' goods. The hour of the sale not being come, they were conversing on the badness of the times; and one of the company called to a plain, clean, old man, with white locks, "Pray, Father Abraham, what think you of the times? Will not these heavy taxes quite ruin the country? How shall we ever be able to pay them? What would you advise us to?" Father Abraham stood up, and replied, "If you would have my Advice, Iwill give it you in short; for A word to the wise is enough., as Poor Richard says." They joined in desiring him to speak his mind, and gathering round him, he proceeded as follows.

 Well, now I have taken you, as the ancient Romans would say of a banquet, ab ovo usque ad mala, from the eggs to the apples (meaning from start to finish). Now, because tempus fugit (time flies), all I have left to say is verbum sat sapienti: a word to the wise is enough.

Urdu	Persian
عمل کے بغیر علم، بے پھل درخت کی مانند ہے /æmæl ki: bə ɣəjrə əlm bi: pəhəl dəræχt ki: mɒ:nænd hə/ *Morovvat, 2007:3.* (معنای برابر فارسی= عالم بی‌عمل مانند درخت بی‌ثمر است) Persian Equivalent Meaning: /ɒ:ləmə bi: æmæl mɒ:nændə dəræχtə bi: sæmær æst/	عالمی را که گفت باشد و بس – هر چه گوید نگیرد اندر کس /ɒ:ləmi: rɒ: kə goft bɒ:ʃæd o bæs/ – /hær t͡ʃə gu:jæd nægi:ræd ændær kæs/ *Dehkhoda, 1984: 1088.*

Proverb's English equivalent: *Example is better than precept*

c **1400** J. MIRK *Festial* (EETS) **216** Then saythe Seynt Austeyn that an ensam-pull yn doyng ys mor commendabull then ys techyng other prechyng.

a **1568** R. ASCHAM *Schoolmaster* (**1570**) I. **20** One example, is more valiable... than xx. preceptes written in bookes.

1708 M. PRIOR *Literary Works* (**1971**) I. **535** Example draws where Precept fails, And Sermons are less read than Tales.

1828 D. M. MOIR *Mansie Wauch* xix. Example is better than precept, as James Batter observes.

1894 J. LUBBOCK *Use of Life* xix. Men can be more easily led than driven: example is better than precept.

<table>
<tr><td align="center">Urdu</td><td align="center">Persian</td></tr>
<tr><td align="center">کل کس نے دیکھی ہے؟
/kæl kæs ni: dəjkhi: hə/
Morovvat, 2007:3.</td><td align="center">فردا را که دیده است؟
/færdɒ: rɒ: kə di:də æst/
Dehkhoda, 1984: 1136.</td></tr>
</table>

Proverb's English equivalent: *Tomorrow never comes*

1523 LD. BERNERS *Froissart* (1901) II. 309 It was sayde every day among them, we shall fight tomorowe, the whiche day came never.

1602 J. CHAMBERLAIN *Letter* 8 May (1939) I. 142 Tomorrow comes not yet.

1678 J. RAY *English Proverbs* (ed. 2) 343 Tomorrow come never.

1756 B. FRANKLIN *Poor Richard's Almanack* (July) To-morrow, every Fault is to be amended; but that To-morrow never comes.

1889 GISSING *Nether World* III. ix. 'It's probably as well for you that to-morrow never comes.' 'Now just see how things turn out!' went on the other.

1966 A. E. LINDOP *I start Counting* xvii. 'It's late, honey. Talk tomorrow.' 'Tomorrow never comes.'

<table>
<tr><td align="center">Urdu</td><td align="center">Persian</td></tr>
</table>

کم کھا ، غم نہ کھا

/kæm kæhɒː ɣæm nə kæhɒː/

Morovvat, 2007:3.

کم بخور همیشه بخور

/kæm bəχor hæmiːʃə bəχor/

Dehkhoda, 1984: 1233.

Proverb's English equivalent: ***A penny saved is a penny earned***

1640 G. HERBERT Outlandish Proverbs no. *506* A penny spar'd is twice got.

a1661 T. FULLER *Worthies* (Hunts.) *51* By the same proportion that a penny saved is a penny gained, the preserver of books is a Mate for the Compiler of them.

1695 E. RAVENSCROFT *Canterbury Guests* II. iv. This I did to prevent expences, for … a penny sav'd, is a penny got.

1748 THOMSON *Castle of Indolence* I. *26* A Penny saved is a Penny got.

1853 CHARLES DICKENS *Bleak House* ix. I saved five pounds out of the brick-maker's affair … It's a very good thing to save one, let me tell you: a penny saved, is a penny got!

1923 P. G. WODEHOUSE *Inimitable Jeeves* xi. I can save money this way; and believe me, laddie, nowadays … a penny saved is a penny earned.

1979 A. LURIE *Only Children 5* You can hear his engine saying the same dull things he said in history -- A penny saved is a pen-ny earned, he said, over and over again.

Urdu	Persian
من میں بسے، دسپنے دسے /mən məjn bæsi: dəspəni: dæsi:/ *Morovvat, 2007:3.* (معنای برابر فارسی= گرسنه در خواب نان سنگک می‌بیند) Persian Equivalent Meaning: /gorosnə dæ χɒ:b nɒ:nə sængæk mi: bi:næd/	مشابه: شتر در خواب بیند پنبه دانه – گهی لپ لپ خورد گه دانه دانه Equivalent: /ʃotor dær χɒ:b bi:næd pænbə dɒ:nə/ – /gæhi: lop lop xoræd gæh dɒ:nə dɒ:nə/ *Dehkhoda, 1984: 1018.*

Proverb's English equivalent: *The wish is father to the thought*

1598 SHAKESPEARE *Hanry* IV, Pt. 2 IV. v. 93, I never thought to hear you speak again. --- Thy wish was father, Harry, to that thought

1783 P. VAN SCHAACK *Letter* 5 Jan. in H. C. Van Schaack Life (1842) 321 My 'wish is father to the thought'.

1860 TROLLOPE *Framley Parsonage* III. xiv. The wish might be father to the thought ... but the thought was truly there.

1940 E. F. BENSON *Final Edition* iii. She spied a smallish man ... walking away from us. The wish was father to the thought. 'Ah, there is Lord Ripon,' she said ... He turned round. It wasn't Lord Ripon at all.

Urdu	Persian
منہ پر اور، پیٹھ پیچھے اور /mənə pər or pi:tə pi:tʃi: or/ *Morovvat, 2007:3.* (معنای برابر فارسی= روبرو جانم جانت، پشت سر کاردم اسختوانت) Persian Equivalent Meaning: /ru:bəru: d͡ʒɒ:næm d͡ʒɒ:næt poʃtə sær kɒ:rdɒ:m ostəχɒ:næt/	مشابه: دو دوزه می‌بازد /do du:zə mi: bɒ:zæd/ *Dehkhoda, 1984: 834.*

Proverb's English equivalent: *To run with the hare and hunt with the hounds*

1546 J. HEYWOOD *Dialogue of Proverbs* I. x. C3 There is no mo1 suche tytifils2 in Englands grounde, To holde with the hare, and run with the hounde.

1580 LILY *Euphues* (Edit John Bartlett), I mean not to run with the Hare and holde with the Hounde.

1909 RAFAEL SABATINI *St. Martin's Summer* Part II He had had no hand in it, one way or the other. He had run with the hare and hunted with the hounds, and neither party could charge him with any lack of loyalty. His admiration and respect for

---

[1] more

[2] scoundrels, knaves; from Titivil, formerly a common name for a demon

Monsieur de Garnache grew enormously. When the rash Parisian had left him that afternoon for the purpose of carrying his message himself to Condillac, Tressan had entertained little hope of ever again seeing him alive.

2002 RUTH PADEL *Hare Hunted, Hare Magic, Hare Tamed* Human beings, who put to their own use the different characteristics which animals evolved for their own benefit, have turned the hare's speed to sport, and bred dogs like the greyhound, with a corresponding turn of speed to pursue it. In greyhound racing, what they run after today is an electric "hare". To run with the hare and hunt with the hounds I stryng to keep on both sides, play a doubel game.

Proverb's English equivalent: ***You cannot run with the hare and hunt with the hounds***

a **1449** LYDGATE *Minor Poems* (EETS) **812** He ... holdeth bothe with hounde and hare.

1694 *Trimmer's Confession of Faith* **1**, I can hold with the Hare, and run with the Hound: Which no Body can deny.

1896 M. A. S. HUME *Courtships of Queen Elizabeth* xii. Leicester, as usual, tried to run with the hare and hunt with the hounds, to retain French bribes and yet to stand in the way of French objects

1975 J. O'FAOLAIN *Women in Wall* v. Clotair's henchmen say: 'You cannot run with the hare and hunt with the hounds.' The peasants have an even chearer way of putting this: 'You cannot', they say,' they say, 'side with the cow and the clover.'

Urdu	Persian
نادان کی دوستی جی کا زیان /nɒːdɒːn kiː dostiː d͡ʒiː kɒː zjɒːn/ *Morovvat, 2007:3.*	دوستی خاله خرسه /duːstiː ə χɒːlə χərsə/ *Dehkhoda, 1984: 837.*

Proverb's English equivalent: ***Don't throw the baby out with the bathwater***

1853 CARLYLE *Nigger Question* (ed. 2) **29** Servants hired for life, or by a contract for a long period, and not easily dissoluble; so and not otherwise would all reasonable mortals, Black and White, wish to hire and to be hired! I invite you to reflect on that; for you will find it true. And if true, it is important for us, in reference to this Negro Question and some others. The Germans say, 'you must empty-out the bathing-tub, but not the baby along with it.' Fling-out your dirty water with all zeal, and set it careering down the kennels; but try if you can keep the little child!

1911 G. B. SHAW *Getting Married* Preface **186** We shall in a very literal sense empty the baby out with the bath by abolishing an institution [marriage] which needs nothing more than a little ... rationalizing to make it ... useful.

1937 M. WARD *Insurrection versus Resurrection* i. In their ardour to get rid of it [old–fashioned apologetic] they' emptied out the baby with the bath–water'.

1979 J. P. YOUNG *Art of Learning to Manage* **91** Do be careful that you don't throw the baby out with the bath water, and find yourself with too many people who lack experience.

Proverb's English equivalent: ***To empty out the baby with the bathwater***

1853 THOMAS CARLYLE 'The Germans say, 'You must empty out the bathing-tub, but not the baby along with it.'

1911 GEORGE BERNARD SHAW *Preface to 'Getting Married'* 'We shall in a very literal sense empty the baby out with the bath.'

1992 WOLFGANG MIEDER, STEWART A.KINGSBURY & KELSIE B. HARDER *A Dictionary of American Proverbs* (Oxford University Press, New York, , Page 33). "Don't throw out the baby with the bathwater".

Proverb's English equivalent: ***To throw out the baby with the bathwater***

1512 THOMAS MURNER *Narrenbeschwörung* which contains as its eighty-first short chapter entitled "Das kindt mit dem bad vß schitten" (To throw the baby out with the bath water).

2004 RON STROM Though he says he understands the reasons for the fees, he thinks the Establishment Clause cases have gotten out of hand. "I don't want to throw out the baby with the bathwater," McCarthy said, "but I think it would resonate with most people. The Establishment Clause cases have gotten silly. We've been doing this for 30 years about everything... it's like the ACLU is going from town to town" looking for things to sue over.

2005 KIM KRAVETS *Congress threatens land trusts* It's time to revise tax regulations, but the Joint committee is "seriously overreaching," Grossi said. "They're throwing the baby out with the bathwater. Their recommendations make it very difficult to use easements as a conservation tool going forward."

Urdu	Persian
نام بلند بہ از بام بلند	مشابه:
/nɒːmə bolænd bəh æz bɒːmə bolænd/	سعدیا مرد نکونام نمیرد هرگز ــ مرده آنست که نامش به نکویی نبرند
Morovvat, 2007:3.	
(معنای برابر فارسی= نام بلند بهتر از بام بلند)	Equivalent:
Persian Equivalent Meaning:	/sæʔdiːɒː mærd ə nəkuːnɒːm næmiːræd hærgəz/ – /mordə ɒːn æst kə nɒːmæʃ bə nəkuːiː næbærænd/
/nɒːmə bolænd bəhtær æz bɒːmə bolænd æst/	*Dehkhoda, 1984: 973.*

Proverb's English equivalent: *He lives long who lives well*

1553 T. WILSON *Art of Rhetoric* 45ᵛ They lyued long enough, that have liued well enough.

1619 W. DRUMMOND *Midnight's Trance* (1951) 29 Who liueth well, liueth long.

1642 T. FULLER *The Holy State and the Profane State* I. vi. If he chance to die young, yet he lives long that lives well.

1861 H. BONAR in *Hymns of Faith & Hope* 2nd Ser. 129 He liveth long who liveth well! All other life is short and vain.

Urdu	Persian
نیم حکیم خطره جان - نیم ملا خطره ایمان	نیم حکیم بلای جان - نیم فقیه بلای ایمان
/niːm hæːkiːm χæːtær ə jɒːn/ – /niːm muːllɒː χæːtær ə iːmɒːn/	/niːm hæːkiːm bæːlɒːjə jɒːn/ – /niːm fæGiːh bæːlɒːjə iːmɒːn/
Morovvat, 2007:3.	*Dehkhoda, 1984: 1877.*

Proverb's English equivalent: ***A little learning is a dangerous thing***

1915 FREDERICK ARTHUR TALBOT *Aeroplanes and Dirigibles of War* Chapter XVII Wireless in Aviation As a result of this disaster endeavours were made to persuade Count Zeppelin to abandon the use of aluminium for the framework of his balloon but they were fruitless, a result no doubt due to the fact that the inventor of the airship of this name has but a superficial knowledge of the various sciences which bear upon aeronautics, and fully illustrates the truth of the old adage that "a little learning is a dangerous thing."

1929 ALEISTER CROWLEY *Moonchild* Chapter IX They had not to walk far before the magician found what he was seeking. Beneath the ruins of the rear compartment were the remains of the late Akbar Pasha. "I wonder how that happened," he said. "However, here is a guess at your epitaph: 'a little learning is a dangerous thing.' I think, Lisa, that we should sup at the Cheval Blanc before we start our walk to Barbizon. It is a long way, especially at night, and we want to cut away to the west so as to avoid Fontainebleau, for the sake of the romance of the thing."

Proverb's English equivalent: ***A little knowledge is a
dangerous thing***

1711 POPE *Essay on Criticism* l. *215* A little Learning is a
dang'rous Thing; Drink deep, or taste not the Pierian[1] Spring.

1829 P. EGAN Boxiana 2nd Ser. II. 4 The sensible idea, that 'A
little learning is a dangerous thing!'

1881 T. H. HUXLEY *Science & Culture* iv. If a little knowledge is
dangerous, where is the man who has so much as to be out of
danger?

1974 T. SHARPE *Porterhouse Blue* xviii. His had been an
intellectual decision founded on his conviction that if a little
knowledge was a dangerous thing, a lot was lethal.

---

[1] of Pieria, a region in Northern Greece regarded as the home of the
Muses

<table>
<tr><td align="center">Urdu</td><td align="center">Persian</td></tr>
<tr><td align="right">وقت ہمیشہ ایک سا نہیں رہتا

/væGt hæməʃæ əjk sɒ: nəhi:n rətɒ:/

Morovvat, 2007:4.</td><td align="right">در همیشه به یک پاشنه نمی‌گردد

/dær hæmi:ʃə bə jək pɒ:ʃnə nəmi: gærdæd/

Dehkhoda, 1984: 801.</td></tr>
</table>

Proverb's English equivalent: ***It is a long lane that has no turning***

1633 *Stationers' Register* (**1877**) IV. **273** (ballad) Long runns that neere turnes.

1670 J. RAY *English Proverbs* **117** It's a long run that never turns.

1732 T. FULLER *Gnomologia* no. **2863** It is a long lane that never turns.

1748 RICHARDSON *Clarissa* IV. xxxii. It is a long lane that has no turning–Do not despise me for my proverbs.

1849 BULWER–LYTTON *Caxtons* III. XVII. i. I wonder we did not run away. But... ' It is a long lane that has no turning.'

1945 F. P. KEYES *River Road* VIII. xxxvii. 'You're through in politics, Gervais. You might just as well face it.'...'It's a long lane that has no turning.

<table>
<tr><td align="center">Urdu</td><td align="center">Persian</td></tr>
<tr><td align="center">ہر شخص کا مزاج مختلف ہوتا ہے

/hær ʃæχs kɒ: məzɒ:d͡ʒ moχtæləf hu:tɒ: hə/</td><td align="center">سلیقه‌ها مختلف است

/sæli:Gə hɒ: moχtæləf æst/</td></tr>
</table>

Proverb's English equivalent: *Tastes differ*

1803 J. DAVIS *Travels in USA* ii. Tastes sometimes differ.

1868 W. COLLINS *Moonstone* I. xv. Tastes differ … I never saw a marine landscape that I admired less.

1924 H. DE SELINCOURT *Cricket Match* iii. It's no use arguing about that … Tastes differ.

1940 J. J. CONNINGTON *Four Defences* xii. Tastes differ. One has to admit it.

Urdu	Persian
یرا کیچڑ میں بھی ہیرا رہتا ہے /jərɒ: ki:t͡ʃər məin bəhi: hi:rɒ: rətɒ: hə/ *Morovvat, 2007:4.* (معنای برابر فارسی= دُر دَرِ خلاب نیز دُر است) Persian Equivalent Meaning: /dorrə dærə χəlɒ:b hæm dor æst/	مشابه: پول است نه جان است که آسان بتوان داد Equivalent: /pu:l æst næ d͡ʒɒ:n æst kə ɒ:sɒ:n bətævɒ:n dɒ:d/ *Dehkhoda, 1984: 516.*

Proverb's English equivalent: *Money has no smell*

1922 A. BENNETT *Mr. Prohack* iii. The associations of the wealth scarcely affected him. He understood in the flesh the deep wisdom of that old proverb … that money has no smell.

1940 R. CHANDLER *Farewell, my Lovely* xxxiv. He punched the cash-register and dropped the bill into the drawer. They say money don't stink. I sometimes wonder.

Urdu	Persian
یاروہی جو بھیڑ میں کام آئے /jærohi̱ dʒo bəhi:r məin̠ kɒ:m ɒ:i:/ *Morovvat, 2007:4.*	دوست آن باشد که گیرد دست دوست /du:st ɒ:n bɒ:ʃæd kə gi:ræd dæst ə du:st/ *Dehkhoda, 1984: 836.*

Proverb's English equivalent: ***A friend in need is a friend indeed***

The Latin phrase of "*Amicus certus in re incerta cernitur*" is in use in Latin literature since the 5th B.C. century.

c **1035** *Durham Proverbs* (**1956**) **10** Æt thearfe man sceal freonda cunnian [friend shall be known in time of need].

a **1400** *Titus & Vespasian* (**1905**) **98**, I shal the save When tyme cometh thou art in nede; Than ogh men frenshep to shewe in dede.

a **1449** LYDGATE *Minor Poems* (EETS) II. **755** Ful weele is him that fyndethe a freonde at neede.

1678 J. RAY *English Proverbs* (ed. **2**) **142** A friend in need is a friend indeed.

1773 R. GRAVES *Spiritual Quixote* II. VIII. xx. (heading) A Friend in Need is a Friend indeed.

1866 C. READE *Griffith Gaunt* III. xv. You came to my side when I was in trouble ... A friend in need is a friend indeed.

1935 E. BELL *Fish on Steeple* iv. If they's one thing I do it's never lay down on my friends. I say a friend in need is a friend indeed.

Urdu	Persian
یار کا غصہ بھٹار کے □ پر /jær kɒː ɣossæ bəhtɒːr kiː uːppər/ *Morovvat, 2007:4.*	زورش به خر نمی‌رسد پالانش را می‌زند /zuːræʃ bə χær nəmiː rəsæd pɒːlɒːnæʃ rɒː miːzænæd/ *Dehkhoda, 1984: 929.*

Proverb's English equivalent: ***He that cannot beat the ass beats the saddle***

R. Fergusson introduced this proverb as an English rooted proverb, but research shows this proverb has Turkish root.

1949 CEDARS OF LEBONAN: *Talmudic Proverbs* Vol. **7** "Rav Nahman said: [This is] like a great palace with many thresholds, so that all who enter become lost and cannot leave the palace. Till a clever man comes and takes a hempen strand and ties... The famous Jewish wit is already present, and in this respect there is a direct line from these proverbs to the Yiddish... The following proverbs, culled from the **2301** proverbs collected and annotated by Bialik and Revenitzky in the sixth volume of their Sefer Ha-Agadah, stand in the Babylonian and Palestinian Talmud as well as in the apocryphal volumes of the same period, alongside the essentially legal and homiletic matter... **174** *Talmudic Proverbs* Scepticism Respect him and suspect him... He who cannot beat the donkey, beats the saddle ...

References:

- Abd al-Jabbar, Falih (2008). *Ayatollahs, sufis and ideologues: state, religion and social movements in Iraq*. University of Virginia.

- Abolghasemi, Mohsen (2011) [Persian Calendar 1390]. *Tarikh e zaban e Farsi (History of the Persian language)*. Sazman e motalee va tadvin e kotob e oloom e ensani e daneshgah ha –SAMT- (The Organization of study and codification of the arts' colleges' books -SAMT-): Tehran, IRAN, p 15 & p. 30.

- Abolhasanizadeh, Vahideh|Mahmood Bijankhan|Carlos Gussenhoven (2012). "The Persian pitch accent and its retention after the focus", *Lingua* 122, 13.

- Abramowicz, Zofia|Serszunowicz, Joanna (2016). "Wealth And Poverty In Polish And Russian Proverbs". 1Oth Interdisciplinary Colloquium on Proverbs, Tavira: ICP 16.

- Akiner, Shirin (2013). *Cultural Change & Continuity* In. Routledge. ISBN: 9781136150340.

- Alamolhoda, Seyyed Morleza (2000). "Phonostatistics and Phonotactics of the Syllable in Modern Persian". *Studia Orientalia*. 89: 14–15. ISSN 0039-3282.

- Arberry, Arthur John (1953). *The Legacy of Persia*, Oxford: Clarendon Press, ISBN: 0198219059.

- Asadi Ṭusi, (1365). *Loḡat-e-foros*, ed. F. Mojtabā'i and ʿA.-A. Ṣādeqi, Tehran.

- Ashraf, Asma (1975). "Design Features of Monolingual Urdu Pedagogical", *Thesis submitted in the partial fulfilment of the requirements for the degree of Doctor of Philosophy in English (Ph.D Linguistics), Department of English, Bahauddin Zakariya University*, Multan, Pakistan.

- Bailey, H. W. (1939). "The Rama Story in Khotanese". *Journal of the American Oriental Society*. 59 (4): 460. doi:10.2307/594480.

- Idem, (1970). "The Ancient Kingdom of Khotan". *British Institute of Persian Studies*. 8: 68.

- Beg, M. K. A. (1996). "Sociolinguistic Perspective of Hindi and Urdu in India", *Bahri Publications*. New Delhi.

- Bell, T. R. (1976). *Sociolinguistics: Goals and Approaches and Problems*. B.T.Batsford. Ltd. Great Britain.

- Bergne, Paul (2007). *The Birth of Tajikistan: National Identity and the Origins of the Republic*. I. B. Tauris. ISBN: 9781845112837.

- Bielmeier, Roland (1989). "Sarmatisch, Alanisch, Jassisch und Altosetisch," in *Rüdiger Schmitt, ed., Compendium linguarum Iranicarum*, Wiesbaden, pp. 236-45.

- de Blois, F. (1997). *Persian Literature. A Bio-Bibliographical Survey, begun by the late C. A. Storey* V. *Poetry of the Pre-Mongol Period*, London.

- Idem, (2006). "Glossary to the New Persian Texts in Manichaean Script," *Dictionary of Manichaean Texts* II. *Texts from Iraq and Iran (Texts in Syriac, Arabic, Persian and Zoroastrian Middle Persian)*, ed. F. de Blois and N. Sims-Williams, Turnhout, pp. 89-114.

- Borjian, Habib (2015). 'Judeo-Iranian Languages", in *Handbook of Jewish Languages, ed. Lily Kahn, Aaron D. Rubin*. Leiden | Boston: Brill.

- Borjian, Maryam (2005). "Bilingualism in Mazandaran: Peaceful Coexistence With Persian". *Languages, Comunities and Education*. Spring 2005. pp. 65-73.

- Boyce, M. (1964). "The Use of Relative Particles in Western Middle Iranian", in *Indo-Iranica. Mélanges présentés à Georg Morgenstierne à l'occasion de son soixante-dixième anniversaire*, ed. G. Redard, Wiesbaden, pp. 28-47.

– Idem, (1968). *Middle Persian Literature, Handbuch der Orientalistik 1*, IV, 2, Leiden: Brill, pp. 31–66.

– Idem, (1983). "Parthian Writings and Literature", in *Yarshatar, Ehsan, The Seleucid, Parthian and Sassanian Periods*. Cambridge History of Iran, Vol. 3(2), Cambridge University Press, pp. 1151–1165, ISBN 0-521-24693-8.

– Idem, (2002). "The Parthians", in *Godrej, Pheroza J., A Zoroastrian Tapestry*. New York: Mapin.

– Campbell, George L.|King, Gareth, eds. (2013). "Persian". *Compendium of the World's Languages* (3rd ed.). Routledge.

– Champion, Selwyn Gurney (1938). Racial Proverbs, A Selection of the World's Proverbs arranged Linguistically. London: Routledge & Kegan Paul Ltd.

– Clauson, Gerard (2002). *Studies in Turkic and Mongolic linguistics*.

– Coughlin, Kathryn M. (2006). "Muslim cultures today: a reference guide," *Greenwood Publishing Group*.

– Datasy, Garsan (1961). *Tarikh e adabiyat e Hindustani, (in Urdu)*. New Delhi: Markaz e elm o zaban.

– Dehkhoda, Ali Akbar (1984) [Persian Calendar: 1363]. *Amsal va hekam* (in Persian), Volumes 1-4. Tehran: Amir Kabir Publication.

– Delacy, Richard (2003). *Teach Yourself Beginner's Urdu Script*, McGraw-Hill Companies.

– Dodge, Bayard (1970). *The Fihrist of al-Nadīm: A Tenth-Century Survey of Islamic Culture*. New York, Columbia University Press, 2 vols. [complete English translation].

– Elfenbein, J. (1988). *Encyclopaedia Iranica*: Vol. III, Fasc. 6, pp. 633-644. Originally Published: December 15.

– Farjam, Abdolhamid (2000) [Persian Calendar: 1379]. *Farhang e zarbolmasalha*. Tehran: Ghatran Publisher.

– Filippone, E. (2011). "The Language of the Qorʾān-e Qods and its Sistanic Dialectal Background," in M. Maggi and P. Orsatti, eds., *The Persian Language in History*, Wiesbaden, pp. 179-235.

– Firuz, Alhaj Firuzuddin (1984). *Firuzoloqat (in Urdu)*. Lahore: Science Private Limited.

– Frye, Richard N. (1984). *Handbuch der Altertumswissenschaft: Alter Orient-Griechische Geschichte-Römische Geschichte*. Band III,7: The History of Ancient Iran. C.H.Beck. p. 29. ISBN: 9783406093975.

– Gershevitch, Ilya (1954). *A Grammar of Manichean Sogdian*. p.1. Oxford: Blackwell.

– Idem, (1983), "Bactrian Literature", in *Yarshater, Ehsan, Cambridge History of Iran*, 3 (2), Cambridge: Cambridge UP, pp. 1250–1258, ISBN: 0511467737.

– Ghanbari, Abdollah (2010) [Persian Calendar: 1389]. *Farhang e zarbolmasalhaye engelisi-farsi*. Tehran: Rahnama.

– Habibian, Simin (2002) *One Thousand and One Persian-English Proverbs*, Third Edition. Bethesda, Maryland: Ibex Publishers.

– Haghshenas, Alimohammad (2009) [Persian Calendar: 1388]. *avashenasi (Phonetic) (in Persian)*. Tehran: Agah.

– Haig, Geoffrey L. J.|Öpengin, Ergin (2015). *Gender in Kurdish: Structural and socio-cultural dimensions*, University of Bamberg, Germany.

– Harmatta, János (1994). *History of Civilizations of Central Asia Volume two: The Development of Sedentary and Nomadic*

Civilizations, 700 B. C. to A.D. 250. UNESCO. ISBN: 9231028464.

– Idem, (1958). Mitteliranisch, *Handbuch der Orientalistik* I, IV, I. Leiden: Brill.

– Idem, (1960). "The Bactrian Inscription" *BSO* (A)S 23, pp. 47-55.

– Haque, A. R. (1982). *Report Study Groups on the Teaching of Languages*, University Grants Commission. Ferozsons. Rawalpindi.

– Hosseini, Seyed Ayat (2014) "The Phonology and Phonetics of Prosodic Prominence in Persian" *Ph.D. Dissertation*, University of Tokyo, p.22f for a review of the literature; also p.35.

– Hunger, H. (1953). "Zum Epilog der Theogonie des Johannes Tzetzez," *Byzntinische Zeitschrift* 46, pp. 302-7.

– Hussain, Sarmad. (2004). "Letter to Sound Rules for Urdu Text to Speech System", in *Proceedings of Workshop on Computational Approaches to Arabic Script-based Languages*, COLING, Geneva, Switzerland.

– Ijaz, Madiha | Hussain, Sarmad. *Corpus Based Urdu Lexicon Development*.

– Jahani, Carina (2005). "The Glottal Plosive: A Phoneme in Spoken Modern Persian or Not?". In *Éva Ágnes Csató; Bo Isaksson; Carina Jahani. Linguistic Convergence and Areal Diffusion: Case studies from Iranian, Semitic and Turkic*. London: Routledge Curzon. pp. 79–96. ISBN: 0415308046.

– Johanson, Lars (2006). *Turkic-Iranian Contact Areas Historical and Linguistic Aspects*. Wiesbaden: Harrassowitz.

- Kachru, Yamuna (2006). *Hindi*. John Benjamins Publishing. ISBN 90-272-3812-X.

- Kashmiri, T. (2003). "Urdu Adab Ki Tareekh, Ibtada Se 1857 Tak. [The History of Urdu Literature]" (in Urdu), *Sang-e-Meel Publications*. Lahore.

- Kaye, Alan Stewart (2004). *Persian Loanwords In English*. San Fransisco: English Today Press.

- Kent, Roland G. (1950), *Old Persian: Grammar, texts, lexicon*. New Haven: American Oriental Society.

- Klaproth, Julius von (1814). *Reise in den Kaukasus und Georgien*, Halle and Berlin, "Kaukasische Sprachen," appendix at the end of vol. 2; tr. F. Shoberl as *Travels in the Caucasus and Georgia*, London.

- Kreyenbroek, Philip G. (1992). "On the Kurdish Language", *a chapter in the book The Kurds: A Contemporary Overview*. London;__New York: Routledge. ISBN: 9780415072656.

- Lazard, Gilbert (1963). *La langue des plus anciens monuments de la prose persane*, Paris.

- Idem, (1964). *Les premiers poètes persans (IXe-Xe siècles). Fragments rassemblés, édités et traduits. I: Introduction et traduction française* II. *Textes persans*, Tehran and Paris.

- Idem, (1966). "L'enclitique nominal *-i* en persan: un ou deux morphèmes?" *BSL* 61/1, pp. 249-64.

- Idem, (1971). *"Pahlavi, Parsi, Dari*: Les langues de l'Iran d'après Ibn-al-Muqaffaʿ," in C. E. Bosworth, ed., *Iran and Islam, in memory of the late Vladimir Minorsky*, Edinburgh, pp. 361-91.

- Idem, (1972). *Persian Grammar: History and State of its Study*. Paris. p. 35.

− Idem, (1975). "The Rise of the New Persian Language," in R. N. Frye, ed., *The Cambridge History of Iran* IV. *The Period from the Arab Invasion to the Saljuqs,* Cambridge, pp. 595-632.

− Lecoq, Pierre (1983). "Aparna". *Encyclopedia Iranica. 1.* Costa Mesa: Mazda Pub.

− Levinson, Von David | Christensen, Karen (2002). *Encyclopedia Of Modern Asia,* Charles Scribner's Sons. Vol. 4.

− Mace, John (1993). *Modern Persian, Teach Yourself.* ISBN: 0844238155.

− Idem, (2003). *Persian Grammar: For reference and revision.* London: RoutledgeCurzon. ISBN: 0700716955.

− MacKenzie | David Neil (1961). "Origins of Kurdish," *TPS*, pp. 68-86.

− Idem, (1967). "Notes on the Transcription of Pahlavi," *BSOAS* 30, pp. 17-29.

− Idem, (1991). "Chorasmia, iii. The Chorasmian Language". *Vol. V, Fasc.*, pp. 517-520.

− Mahootian, Shahrzad (1997). *Persian.* London: Routledge. pp. 287, 292, 303, 305. ISBN: 0415023114.

− Manser, Martin H. (2007). *The Facts on File Dictionary of Proverbs*, Associate Editors: Rosalind Fergusson, David Pickering. An imprint of infobase publishing.

− Mansoor, S. (1993). "Punjabi, Urdu, English in Pakistan". *Vanguard. Lahore*, Karachi, Islamabad.

− Masson, Vadim Mikhaïlovich (1992). [Editors, A.H. Dani, V.M. History of civilizations of Central Asia. Paris: *UNESCO.* ISBN: 9231032119.

- Mawr, E B (1885). *Analogous Proverbs In Ten Languages* (Reprint ed. 2005). Kessinger Publishing, LL. ISBN: 9781417964673; ASIN: 1417964677.

- Maze Poua, Ulena (2003). [Persian Calendar: 1382]. "chand molaheze dar mored e tadris e zaban e farsi be Farsiamozam e Ukraini va taelif e ketabhaye zaban e Farsi baraye kharejian (in Persian)", Tehran: *Sokhan e Eshgh [magazine]*. NO: 20.

- Meier, F. (1981). "Aussprachefragen des älteren Neupersisch," *Oriens* 27-28, pp. 70-176.

- Meshkatoddini, Mahdi (1985) [Persian Calendar: 1364]. *sakhte avaei e zaban (in Persian)*. Mashhad: Naneshgah e Ferdowsi.

- Mirza, Hormazdyar Kayoji (2002). "Literary treasures of the Zoroastrian priests", in *Godrej, Pheroza J., A Zoroastrian Tapestry*, New York: Mapin, pp. 162–163.

- Modarresi Ghavvami, Golnaz (2011) [Persian Calendar: 1390]. *avashenasi barrasi e elmi e goftar (in Persian)*. Tehran: Samt.

- Morgenstierne, G. (1927). *An Etymological Vocabulary Of Pashto*, Oslo.

- Idem, (1930). "The Waṇetsi Dialect Of Pashto," *Nts 4*, 1930, pp. 156-75.

- Idem, (1982). "Afghanistan Vi. Pashto," Encyclopaedia Iranica, *Vol. I, Fasc. 5, pp. 516-522. Online Edition. Available At: Http://Www.Iranicaonline.Org/Articles/Afghanistan-Vi-Pasto.*

- Morovvat, Gholam (2007). "Urdu aur farsi mein mohaverat ka eshterak" (in Urdu). *Khayaban Magazine*, Peyshavar: Jame-ehye-Peyshavar.

- Naqavi, Seyed Qodrat (1988). *Moqtadarah qomi zaban (in Urdu)*. Islamabad: Lesani Maqalat.

- Nasidze, Ivan|Quinque, Dominique|Rahmani, Manijeh|Alemohamad, Seyed Ali|Stoneking, Mark (2006). "Concomitant Replacement of Language and mtDNA in South Caspian Populations of Iran". *Current Biology*. 16 (7): 668–673.

- Németh, J. (1958). "Die Jassen in Ungarn", *Abh. der deutschen Akademie der Wissenschaften*, no. 4.

- Novák, Ľubomir (2014). "Question of (re)classification of Eastern Iranian languages". *Linguistica Brunensia*: 77–87.

- Numan, Muhammad (2009). *Proposal of Inclusion of Certain Characters in Unicode*, Pakistan: Chishti Iqbal Academy.

- Ohala, Manjari (1999), "Hindi", in *International Phonetic Association, Handbook of the International Phonetic Association: a Guide to the Use of the International Phonetic Alphabet*, Cambridge University Press, pp. 100–103, ISBN 978-0-521-63751-0.

- O'Kane, B. (2009). *The Appearance of Persian on Islamic Art*, New York.

- Pahlavan, Changiz (1996) [Persian Calendar: 1375]. "zaban e Farsi dar jahan e emrooz (in Persian)", Tehran: *Kelk [magazine]*. NO: 75.

- Pandit, P.B. (1977). *Language in a plural society: The Case of India*. Dev Raj Chanana Memorial Committee. New Delhi.

- Parsinejad, Iraj (2003). *A History of Literary Criticism in Iran*, 1866-1951, Ibex Publishers.

- Paul, Ludwig (2002). "A Linguist's Fresh View on 'Classical Persian'," in M. Szuppe, ed., *Iran. Questions et connaissances. Actes du IVe Congrès Européen des Études*

Iraniennes, organisé par la Societas Iranologica Europaea, Paris, 6-10 Septembre 1999 II.*Périodes médiévale et moderne*, Paris, pp. 21-34.

– Idem, (2008). "Kurdish language I. History of the Kurdish language". In *Yarshater, Ehsan. Encyclopædia Iranica.* London and New York: Routledge. Archived from the original on 4 December 2011. Retrieved 28 August 2013.

– Idem, (2009). "Remarks on the Evolution and Distribution of the New Persian Adjectival Suffixes -*īn* and -*ī*," in C. Allison, A. Joisten-Pruschke, and A. Wendtland, eds., *From Daēnā to Dîn. Religion, Kultur und Sprache in der iranischen Welt. Festschrift für Philip Kreyenbroek zum 60. Geburtstag*, Wiesbaden, pp. 105-10.

– Idem, (2013). *A Grammar of Early Judeo-Persian*, Wiesbaden.

– Idem, (2018). (Last Updated: November 19, 2013). *Persian Language i. Early New Persian*: http://www.iranicaonline.org/articles/persian-language-1-early-new-persian.

– Pereira Da Silva Nunes, Leila (2016). "Proverbs And Collective Memory – A Walking Tour Through The Language-Ethnological Atlas Of Southern Brazil". 1Oth Interdisciplinary Colloquium on Proverbs, Tavira: ICP 16.

– Perry, J. R. (1991). *Form and Meaning in Persian Vocabulary. The Arabic Feminine Ending.* Costa Mesa, Cal.

– Platts, J. J. (2005). "Urdu Klasiky Hindi aur Angrizi Dekshenery (in Urdu)". Lahore: *Urdu Science Board.*

– Postgate, J. N. (2007). "Languages of Iraq, ancient and modern", *British School of Archaeology in Iraq*, [Iraq]: British School of Archaeology in Iraq, p. 138.

– Pisowicz, A. (1985). *Origins of the New and Middle Persian Phonological Systems*, Krakow.

– Qazvini, M. (1953) [Persian Calendar: 1332]. "Moqaddama-ye qadim-e Šāhnāma," in idem, *Bist maqāla* II, Tehran, pp. 1-64.

– Rahman, T. (1997). "The Medium of Instruction Controversy in Pakistan". *Journal of Multilingual and Multicultural Development*, Vol. 18, No. 2.

– Rahmandoost, Mostafa (2008) [Persian Calendar: 1387]. *foot e kouzegari va dstanhay e aan (in Persian)*, Second Version. Tehran: Masreseh Publicatiopn.

– Ravāqi, A. (1984) [Persian Calendar: 1363]. ed., *Qorʾān-e Qods. Kohantarin bargardān-e Qorʾān ba fārsi*, Tehran.

– Rees, Daniel A. (2008). "From Middle Persian to Proto-Modern Persian". *Towards Proto-Persian: An Optimality Theoretic Historical Reconstruction* (Ph.D).

– Reza, Enayatollah (2010) [Persian Calendar: 1387]. "Nam e daryay e shomal", *Markaz e daeratolmaaref e bozorg e eslami/Markaz e pazhouhesh haye Irani va Eslami*: Tehran, IRAN, p 107.

– Ridout, Ronald & Witting, Clifford (2009) [Persian Calendar: 1388]. *English Proverbs Explained*. Translated into Persian Zarbolmasalha; engelisi be farsi va farsi be engelisi by Hamid Reza Balouch & Masoud Mirzaei. Tehran: Payk e farhang.

– Rypka J. (1968). et al., *History of Iranian Literature*, Dordrecht.

– Sadat-Tehrani, Nima (2007). "The Intonational Grammar of Persian". *Ph.D. Thesis*, University of Manitoba, pp. 3, 22, 46-47, 51.

– Ṣādeqi A.-A. (1978)) [Persian Calendar: 1357]. *Takwin-e zabān-e fārsi*, Tehran.

xi

- Samareh, Yadollah (1985) [Persian Calendar: 1364]. *avashenani e zaban e farsi (in Persian)*. Tehran: Markaz e nashr e daneshgahi.

- Scott, Cameron Levi|Sela, Ron (2010). *Islamic Central Asia: An Anthology of Historical Sources*. Indiana University Press. ISBN: 0253353858.

- Serszunowicz, Joanna (2016). "Proverbial Expressions In Brand Image Building, A Case Study Of The Polish Beer Brand Zubr Commercials". 1Oth Interdisciplinary Colloquium on Proverbs, Tavira: ICP 16.

- Shebli, Mohammad Seddiq (1997). *Taesir e Zaban e Farsi bar Urdu* . Islamabad: Markaz e Tahqiqat e Farsi Iran va Pakestan.

- Simpson, John (1985). *The Concise Oxford Dictionary of Proverbs*. Oxford New York: Oxford University Press.

- Spooner, Brian (1994). "Dari, Farsi, and Tojiki". in *Marashi, Mehdi. Persian Studies in North America: Studies in Honor of Mohammad Ali Jazayery*. Leiden: Brill. pp. 177–178.

- Idem, (2012). "Dari, Farsi, and Tojiki". in *Schiffman, Harold. Language policy and language conflict in Afghanistan and its neighbors: the changing politics of language choice*. Leiden: Brill. p. 94.

- Strauss, Emanuel (1994). *Dictionary of European proverbs* (Volume 2 ed.). Routledge. p. 878. ISBN: 0415096243.

- Sundermann, W. (1986). "Studien zur kirchengeschichtlichen Literatur der iranischen *Manichäer II," AoF 13*, pp. 241-319.

- Idem, (1989). "Mittelpersisch," in *ed. R. Schmitt, ed., Compendium Linguarum Iranicarum*, Wiesbaden, pp. 138-164.

- *Tārik̲-e Sistān*, (1935) [Persian Calendar: 1314]. ed. M. Bahār, Tehran,; repr., (2010) [Persian Calendar: 1389].

- Teixeira, Jose (2016). "More Important Than The Truth: The Argumentative Value Of Proverbs". *1Oth Interdisciplinary Colloquium on Proverbs*, Tavira: ICP 16.

- Thackston, W. M. (1993). "Colloquial Transformations". An Introduction To Persian (3rd Rev Ed.). *Ibex Publishers*. pp. 205–214. ISBN: 0936347295.

- Idem, (2006). *Kurmanji Kurdish: A Reference Grammar With Selected Readings*.

- Thordarson, Fridrik (1989). "Ossetic," in *Rüdiger Schmitt, Ed., Compendium Linguarum Iranicarum*, Wiesbaden, pp. 456-479.

- Idem, (Last Updated: July 20, 2009). *Ossetic Language I. History And Description*: http://Www.Iranicaonline.Org/Articles/Ossetic.

- Toosravandani, Maziar D. (2004). "Vowel Length In Modern Farsi", *JRAS*, Series 3, 14, 3, pp. 241–251.

- Vrzić, Zvjezdana (2007). *Farsi: A Complete Course for Beginners, Living Language*, Random House. ISBN: 9781400023479.

- Waghmar, Burzine K. (2001) "Bactrian History and Language: An Overview." *Journal of the K. R. Cama Oriental Institute*, 64. pp. 40–48.

- Windfuhr, Gernot L. (1975), "Isoglosses: A Sketch On Persians And Parthians, Kurds And Medes", *Monumentum H.S. Nyberg Ii (Acta Iranica-5)*, Leiden: 457-471.

- Idem, (1979). "Persian grammar: History and State of its Study." *Mouton*. ISBN: 9027977747.

- Idem, (1989). *New Iranian Languages: Overview.* In Rüdiger Schmitt, Ed., Compendium Linguarum Iranicarum. Wiesbaden: L. Reichert.

- Idem, (2009). Ed., *The Iranian Languages.* Routledge.

- Ylliet, Aicka|Kapo, Bisej (2016). "Symbolic Representation And Socio-Cultural Meaning In The Binomial Game Proverb-Slogans In Literature, Journalism, Cinematography Under The Method Of Socialist Realism In The Works Of Enver Hoxha". 1Oth Interdisciplinary Colloquium on Proverbs, Tavira: ICP 16.

- Yousefi, Hadi (2012). "Comparative Study of Culture in Kurdish and Farsi Proverbs". *Macrothink Institute:* International Journal of Learning & Development ISSN 21644063 2012, Vol. 2, No. 6.

- Zarrinkoub, Abdolhossein (1959). *naqde adabi,* pp: 374–379.

- Zarshenas, Zohreh (1988) [Persian Calendar: 1367]. Madkhal e Iran (Entry: Iran). Daeratolmaaref e bozorg e eslami. *Markaz e daeratolmaaref e bozorg e eslami,* v. 10: Tehran, IRAN, p 557.

سرشناسه:	**عابدیان کاسگری، علی اکبر، ۱۳۳۷ –**
	Abedian Kasgari, Ali Akbar
عنوان و نام پدیدآور	Persian proverbs' effects on Urdu language: a paremiologic research / A. A. Abedian K. Edited by: Morvarid Abedian Kasgari
مشخصات نشر:	تهران: دگراندیشان، ۱۳۹۶- ۲۰۱۷م.
شابک:	9781979549059
وضعیت فهرست-	فیپا
یادداشت	انگلیسی
یادداشت	عنوان به فارسی: تاثیر ضرب المثل های فارسی بر زبان اردو.
یادداشت	کتابنامه.
آوانویسی عنوان	پرشین ...
موضوع	فارسی — تاثیر بر اردو
موضوع	Persian language -- Influence on Urdu
موضوع	ضرب‌المثل‌های فارسی
موضوع	Proverbs, Persian
موضوع	ضرب‌المثل‌های اردو
موضوع	Proverbs, Urdu
شناسه افزوده	عابدیان کاسگری، مروارید، ۱۳۷۶ - ، ویراستار
شناسه افزوده	Abedian Kasgari, Morvarid
رده‌بندی کنگره	PK۱۳۹۷/ ع۲پ۴ ۱۳۹۶
رده‌بندی دیویی	۴۹۱ / ۴۳۹
شماره کتابشناسی ملی	۴۹۳۱۵۷۴

ناشر: موسسه انتشارات دگراندیشان

تهران: صندوق پستی ۱۹۵۷۵/۵۷۱

همه حقوق محفوظ است.

تأثیر ضرب المثل های فارسی

بر زبان اردو

ع. الف. عابدیان